Lessons in Life

For All Who Will Read Them

T. S. Arthur

Alpha Editions

This edition published in 2022

ISBN : 9789356719002

Design and Setting By
Alpha Editions
www.alphaedis.com
Email - info@alphaedis.com

Contents

PREFACE. ....- 1 -

THE RIGHT OF WAY. ....- 2 -

COALS OF FIRE. ....- 13 -

A NEW PLEASURE. ....- 23 -

THE DAUGHTER-IN-LAW. ....- 32 -

SMITH AND JONES; OR, THE TOWN
LOT. ....- 48 -

HE MUST HAVE MEANT ME. ....- 56 -

FOR THE FUN OF IT. ....- 68 -

FORGIVE AND FORGET. ....- 79 -

PAYING THE MINISTER. ....- 87 -

HAD I BEEN CONSULTED. ....- 99 -

THE MISTAKES OF A "RISING
FAMILY." ....- 108 -

THE MEANS OF ENJOYMENT ....- 118 -

PREFACE.

"WE are never too old to learn;" is a truism that cannot be repeated too often, if, in the repetition, we do not lose the force of the sentiment. In fact, at every stage of existence we are learners; and, if we (sic) con the lessons well that are written in the great Book of Human Life, wide open before us, we will be wiser and happier. To make the study easier for some, the Stories in this little volume have been written. They present a few marked phases in life, and the lessons taught are worthy of thoughtful consideration.

"STORIES FOR PARENTS" will speedily follow this volume, and make the eighth in our "LIBRARY FOR THE HOUSEHOLD."

THE RIGHT OF WAY.

MR. EDWARD BOLTON had purchased himself a farm, and taken possession thereof. Once, while examining the premises, before deciding to buy, he had observed a light wagon moving along on the extreme south edge of the tract of land included in the farm, but it had occasioned no remark. It was late in the afternoon when he arrived with his family at their new home. On the morning that followed, while Mr. Bolton stood conversing with a farm-hand who had been on the place under the former owner, he observed the same vehicle passing across the portion of his land referred to.

"Whose wagon is that, Ben?" he asked, in the tone of a man who felt that another had trespassed upon his rights.

"It is Mr. Halpin's," was replied.

"Halpin, who owns the next farm?"

"Yes, sir."

"He takes a liberty with my premises that I would not like to take with his," said Mr. Bolton, who was annoyed by the circumstance. "And there he is himself, as I live! riding along over my ground as coolly as if it belonged to him. Verily, some men have the impudence of old Nick himself!"

"They always go by that road," replied Ben; "at least, it has been so ever since I have worked on the farm. I think I once heard Mr. Jenkins, from whom you bought, tell somebody that Mr. Halpin's farm had the right of way across this one.

"The right of way across my farm!" exclaimed Mr. Bolton, with strongly-marked surprise. "We'll see about that! Come! go with me. I want to take a look at that part of my forty acres."

And Mr. Bolton strode off, accompanied by Ben, to take more particular note of the extreme south edge of his beautiful tract of land. The shape of this tract was somewhat in the form of a triangle, with the apex at the southern boundary, near the verge of which ran a stream of water. Beyond this stream was a narrow strip of ground, some thirty feet wide, bounded by the fence enclosing the land belonging to another owner; (sic) it length was not more than two hundred feet. It was along this strip of ground that Mr. Bolton had observed the wagon of Mr. Halpin pass. The gate opening upon his premises was at one end, and now, for the first time, he discovered that there was a gate at the other end, opening from his farm to that of Mr. Halpin, while the ground was cut up with numerous wheel-tracks.

"Upon my word, this is all very fine!" said Mr. Bolton. "The right of way across my farm! we'll see about that! Ben, do you get four good rails and put them firmly into the gate-posts on Mr. Halpin's side. Throw the gate over into his field."

Ben looked confounded at this order.

"Do you understand me?" said Mr. Bolton.

"Yes, sir; but"—

"But what?"

"There's no other way for Mr. Halpin's folks to get to the public road."

"That's none of my business; they've no right to make a public highway of these premises. You heard what I said?"

"Yes, sir."

"Then let it be done."

"Obey orders, if you break owners," muttered Ben, as Mr. Bolton turned and marched away with long and hasty strides. "But if there isn't a nice tea-party somewhere about these diggins before to-morrow morning, my name isn't Ben Johnson."

Before reaching his house, Mr. Bolton's excitement had cooled a trifle, and it came into his mind that *possibly* he might have acted a *little* hastily; but the order had been given to cut off the right of way, and he was not the man to "make back-tracks" in any thing.

"Do you see that, Edward?" said Mrs. Bolton, as her husband entered the house, pointing to a table on which stood a pitcher of sweet cream and two pounds of fresh butter. "Mrs. Halpin sent these over, with her compliments, this morning; isn't it kind in her?"

Mrs. Bolton's countenance was glowing with pleasure.

"I always heard that she was a neighbourly, good woman," added Mrs. Bolton.

"I don't think much of her husband," returned Mr. Bolton, coldly, as he passed from the room after pausing there for only a moment. He could not look at the lumps of golden butter and the pitcher of cream without feeling rebuked, and so he got away as quickly as possible.

"Have you done as I directed?" said Mr. Bolton, with knit brows, on meeting Ben, some time afterwards, returning from the part of the farm where he had left him.

"Yes, sir," was the answer of Ben.

"What did you do with the gate?"

"I threw it into the field, as you told me."

"You didn't break it?"

"No, sir."

"Very well."

"There'll be trouble, Mr. Bolton," said Ben.

"How do you know?"

"Mr. Halpin's a very determined man."

"So am I," replied Mr. Bolton.

"Mr. Dix says the right of way belongs to Mr. Halpin, and no mistake."

"When did he say so?"

"Just now. He came down from his house, when he saw me at work, and asked what I was doing; and when I told him, he said you were wrong, and would only get yourself into trouble; that Mr. Halpin's farm had the right of way through yours."

"Tell Mr. Dix, when you see him again, not to meddle in my affairs," replied Mr. Bolton. "I am entirely competent to manage them myself; I want no assistance."

As Mr. Bolton turned from Ben, on uttering this speech, he saw Mr. Dix, who owned another farm that adjoined his, approaching the place where he stood.

"I want none of his interference," muttered Bolton to himself. Then forcing a smile into his face, he met his neighbour with a pleasant greeting.

"You will excuse me," said Mr. Dix, after a few words had passed between them, "for a liberty I am about to take. I saw your man, a little while ago, closing up the gate that opens from your farm into Mr. Halpin's."

"Well!" Mr. Bolton's brows contracted heavily.

"Are you aware that his farm has the right of way through yours?"

"No, sir."

"Such, however, let me assure you, is the case. Mr. Halpin has no other avenue to the public road."

"That's his misfortune; but it gives him no license to trespass on my property."

"It is not a trespass, Mr. Bolton. He only uses a right purchased when he bought his farm, and one that he can and will sustain in the courts against you."

"Let him go to court, then. I bought this farm for my own private use, not as a highway; no such qualification is embraced in the deed. The land is mine, and no one shall trespass upon it."

"But, Mr. Bolton," calmly replied the other, "in purchasing, you secured an outlet to the public road."

"Certainly I did; but not through your farm, nor that of any one else."

"Halpin was not so fortunate," said Mr. Dix. "In buying his farm, he had to take it with a guarantied right of way across this one. There was no other outlet."

"It was not a guarantee against my ownership," doggedly replied Mr. Bolton.

"Pardon me for saying that in this you are in error," returned the other. "Originally both farms were in one; that was subsequently sold with a right of way across this."

"There is no such concession in the deed I hold," said Bolton.

"If you will take the trouble to make an examination in the clerk's office in the county court, you'll find it to be as I state."

"I don't care any thing about how it was originally," returned Bolton, with the headiness of passionate men when excited. "I look only to how it is now. This is my farm; I bought it with no such concessions, and will not yield it unless by compulsion. I wouldn't be the owner of a piece of land that another man had the right to enter."

"That little strip of ground," said Mr. Dix, "which is of but trifling value, might be fenced off as a road. This would take away all necessity for entering your ground."

"What!" said Bolton, indignantly; "vacate the property I have bought and paid for? I am not quite so generous as that. If Mr. Halpin must have a right of way, let him obtain his right by purchase. I'll sell him a strip from off the south side of my farm, wide enough for a road, if that will suit him; but he shall not use one inch of my property as a common thoroughfare."

Mr. Dix still tried to argue the matter with Bolton, but the latter had permitted himself to get angry, and angry men are generally deaf as an adder to the voice of reason. So the neighbour, who called in the hope of turning the new occupant of the farm from his purpose, and thus saving trouble to both himself and Mr. Halpin, retired without effecting what he wished to accomplish.

It would be doing injustice to the feelings of Mr. Bolton to say, that he did not feel some emotions of regret for his precipitate action. But, having assumed so decided a position in the matter, he could not think of retracing a step that he had taken. Hasty and positive men are generally weak-minded, and this weakness usually shows itself in a pride of consistency. If they say a thing, they will persevere in doing it, right or wrong, for fear that others may think them vacillating, or, what they really are, weak-minded. Just such a man was Mr. Bolton.

"I've said it, and I'll do it!" That was one of his favourite expressions. And he repeated it to himself, now, to drive off the repentant feelings that came into his mind.

At dinner-time, when Mr. Bolton sat down to the table, he found, placed just before him, a print of the golden butter sent to his wife on that very morning by Mrs. Halpin. The sight annoyed and reproved him. He felt that he had been hasty, unneighbourly, and, it might be, unjust; for, as little gleams of reflection came breaking in one after another upon his mind, he saw that a right of way for Mr. Halpin was indispensable, and that if his deed gave it to him, it was a right of which he could not deprive him without acting unjustly. Passion and false reasonings would, it is true, quickly darken his mind again. But they had, in turn, to give place to more correct views and feelings.

"Just try some of that butter. It is delicious!" said Mrs. Bolton, soon after they were seated at the table.

"I don't care about butter at dinner-time," replied Mr. Bolton, coldly.

"But just try some of this. I want you to taste it," urged the wife. "Its flavour is delightful. I must go over and see Mrs. Halpin's dairy."

To satisfy his wife, Mr. Bolton took some of the butter on his plate. He would rather have thrown it out of the window.

"Now try it on a piece of bread," said Mrs. Bolton. "I declare! You act as if you were afraid of the butter. What's the matter with you?"

There was no reason why Mr. Bolton should not do as his wife wished—at least no reason that he could give to her. It wouldn't do to say—

"I won't touch Mrs. Halpin's butter because I've cut off her husband's right of way across my land. I have nailed up the only outlet there is from his property to the public road."

No, it wouldn't do to say that. So, nothing was left for Mr. Bolton but to taste the delicious butter.

"Isn't it very fine?" said his wife, as she saw him place it to his lips.

"Yes, it's good butter," replied Mr. Bolton, "very good butter." Though, in fact, it was far from tasting pleasant to him.

"It's more than very good," said Mrs. Bolton, impatiently. "What has come over you? But wait a little while, and I'll give you something to quicken your palate. I've made some curds—you are so fond of them. If you don't praise the sweet cream Mrs. Halpin so kindly sent over this morning, when you come to eat these curds, I shall think—I don't know what I shall think."

The dinner proceeded, and, at length, the dessert, composed of curds and cream, was served.

"Isn't that beautiful?" said Mrs. Bolton, as she poured some of the cream received from Mrs. Halpin into a saucer of curds, which she handed to her husband.

Bolton took the curds and ate them. Moreover, he praised the cream; for, how could he help doing so? Were not his wife's eyes on him, and her ears open? But never in his life had he found so little pleasure in eating.

"Do you know," said Mrs. Bolton, after she had served the curds and said a good deal in favour of the cream, "that I promise myself much pleasure in having such good neighbours? Mrs. Halpin I've always heard spoken of in the highest terms. She's a sister of Judge Caldwell, with whose family we were so intimate at Haddington."

"You must be in error about that."

"No. Mrs. Caldwell often spoke to me about her, and said that she had written to her sister that we talked of buying this farm."

"I never knew this before," said Mr. Bolton.

"Didn't you! I thought I had mentioned it."

"No."

"Well it's true. And, moreover, Mrs. Caldwell told me, before we left, that she had received a letter from her sister, in which she spoke of us, and in which she mentioned that her husband had often heard you spoken of by the judge, and promised himself great pleasure in your society."

Mr. Bolton pushed back his chair from the table, and, rising, left the room. He could not bear to hear another word.

"Is my horse ready, Ben?" said he, as he came into the open air.

"Yes, sir," replied Ben.

"Very well. Bring him round."

"Are you going now?" asked Mrs. Bolton, coming to the door, as Ben led up the horse.

"Yes. I wish to be home early, and so must start early."

And Bolton sprang into the saddle.

But for the presence of his wife, it is more than probable that he would have quietly directed Ben to go and rehang the gate, and thus re-establish Mr. Halpin's right of way through his premises. But, this would have been an exposure of himself to his better-half that he had not the courage to make. So he rode away. His purpose was to visit the city, which was three miles distant, on business. As he moved along in the direction of the gate through which he was to pass on his way to the turnpike, he had to go very near the spot where Ben had been at work in the morning. The unhinged gate lay upon the ground where, according to his directions, it had been thrown; and the place it formerly occupied was closed up by four strong bars, firmly attached to the posts.

Mr. Bolton didn't like the looks of this at all. But it was done; and he was not the man to look back when he had once undertaken to do a thing.

As he was riding along, just after passing from his grounds, he met Mr. Dix, who paused as Bolton came up.

"Well, neighbour," said the former in a tone of mild persuasion, "I hope you have thought better of the matter about which we were talking a few hours ago."

"About Halpin's right of way through my farm, you mean?"

"Yes. I hope you have concluded to reopen the gate, and let things remain as they have been, at least for the present. These offensive measures only provoke anger, and never do any good." Bolton shook his head.

"He has no right to trespass on my premises," said he, sternly.

"As to the matter of right," replied Mr. Dix, "I think, the general opinion will be against you. By attempting to carry out your present purpose, you will subject yourself to a good deal of odium; which every man ought to avoid, if possible. And in the end, if the matter goes to court, you will not only have to yield this right of way, but be compelled to pay costs of suit and such damages as may be awarded against you for expense and trouble occasioned Mr. Halpin. Now let me counsel you to avoid all these consequences, if possible."

"Oh, you needn't suppose all this array of consequences will frighten me," said Mr. Bolton. "I don't know what fear is. I generally try to do right, and then, like Crockett, 'go ahead.'"

"Still, Mr. Bolton," urged the neighbour mildly, "don't you think it would be wiser and better to see Mr. Halpin first, and explain to him how much you are disappointed at finding a right of way for another farm across the one you have purchased? I am sure some arrangement, satisfactory to both, can be made. Mr. Halpin, if you take him right, is not an unreasonable man. He'll do almost any thing to oblige another. But he is very stubborn if you attempt to drive him. If he comes home and finds things as they now are, he will feel dreadfully outraged; and you will become enemies instead of friends."

"It can't be helped now," said Mr. Bolton. "What's done is done."

"It's not yet too late to undo the work," suggested Mr. Dix.

"Yes, it is. I'm not the man to make back-tracks. Good-day, Mr. Dix?"

And speaking to his horse, Mr. Bolton started off at a brisk trot. He did not feel very comfortable. How could he? He felt that he had done wrong, and that trouble and mortification were before him. But a stubborn pride would not let him retrace a few wrong steps taken from a wrong impulse. To the city he went, transacted his business, and then turned his face homeward, with a heavy pressure upon his feelings.

"Ah me!" he sighed to himself, as he rode along. "I wish I had thought twice this morning before I acted once. I needn't have been so precipitate. But I was provoked to think that any one claimed the right to make a public road through my farm. If I'd only known that Halpin was a brother-in-law to Judge Caldwell! That makes the matter so much worse."

And on rode Mr. Bolton, thinking only of the trouble he had so needlessly pulled down about his ears.

For the last mile of the way, there had been a gentleman riding along in advance of Mr. Bolton, and as the horse of the latter made a little the best speed, he gained on him slowly, until, just as he reached the point where the road leading to his farm left the turnpike, he came up with him.

"Mr. Bolton, I believe," said the gentleman, smiling, as both, in turning into the narrow lane, came up side by side.

"That is my name," was replied.

"And mine is Halpin," returned the other, offering his hand, which Mr. Bolton could but take, though not so cordially as would have been the case had the gate opening from his farm into Mr. Halpin's been on its hinges. "I have often heard my brother-in-law, Judge Caldwell, speak of you and your lady. We promise ourselves much pleasure in having you for neighbours. Mrs. Halpin and I will take a very early opportunity to call upon you. How is all your family?"

"Quite well, I thank you," replied Mr. Bolton, trying to appear polite and pleased, yet half averting his face from the earnest eyes of Mr. Halpin.

"We have had a beautiful day," said the latter, who perceived that, from some cause, Mr. Bolton was not at ease.

"Very beautiful," was the brief answer.

"You have been into the city," said Mr. Halpin, after a brief pause.

"Yes, I had some business that made it necessary for me to go into town."—Another silence.

"You have a beautiful farm. One of the finest in the neighbourhood," said Mr. Halpin.

"Yes, it is choice land," returned the unhappy Mr. Bolton.

"The place has been a little neglected since the last occupant left," continued Mr. Halpin. "And since your purchase of it, some ill-disposed persons have trespassed on the premises. Day before yesterday, as I was passing along the lower edge of your farm,—you know that, through some ill-contrivance, my right of way to the public road is across the south edge of your premises. But we will talk of that some other time. It's not a good arrangement at all, and cannot but be annoying to you. I shall make some proposition, before long, about purchasing a narrow strip of ground and fencing it in as a road. But of that another time. We shall not quarrel about it. Well, as I was saying, day before yesterday, as I was passing along the lower edge of your farm, I saw a man deliberately break a large branch from a choice young plum-tree, in full blossom, near your house, that only came into bearing last year. I was terribly vexed about it, and rode up to remonstrate with him. At first, he seemed disposed to resent my interference with his right to destroy my neighbour's property. But, seeing that I was not in a temper to be trifled with, he took himself off. I then went back home, and sent one of my lads over, in company with a couple of good dogs, and put the property in their charge. I found all safe when I returned in the evening."

"It was kind in you—very kind!" returned Mr. Bolton. He could say no less. But, oh! how rebuked and dissatisfied he felt.

"About that right of way," he stammered out, after a brief silence, partly averting his eyes as he spoke. "I—I"—

"Oh, we'll not speak of that now," returned Mr. Halpin cheerfully. "Let's get better acquainted first."

"But, Mr. Halpin—I—I"—

They were now at the gate entering upon Mr. Bolton's farm, and the neighbour pushed it open, and held it for Bolton to pass through. Then, as it swung back on its hinges, he said, touching his hat politely—

"Good-day! Mrs. Halpin and I will call over very soon;—perhaps this evening, if nothing interfere to prevent. If we come, we shall do so without any ceremony. Make my compliments, if you please, to Mrs. Bolton."

"Thank you! Yes—yes! Mr. Halpin—I—I—Let me speak a—a"—

But Mr. Halpin had turned his horse's head, and was moving off towards the place of entrance to his own farm.

Poor Bolton What was he to do? Never had he felt so oppressive a sense of shame—such deep humiliation. He had reined up his horse after passing through the gate, and there he still stood, undetermined, in the confusion of the moment, what to do. Briskly rode Mr. Halpin away; and only a few moments would pass before he discovered the outrage perpetrated against him, and that by a man for whom he had entertained the kindest feelings in advance, and even gone out of his way to serve.

"Oh, why did I act with such mad haste!" exclaimed Mr. Bolton, as he thought this, and saw but a moment or two intervening between him and the bitterest humiliation. He might repair the wrong, and, in his heart, he resolved to do it. But what could restore to him the good opinion of his neighbour? Nothing! That was gone for ever.

So troubled, oppressed, and shame-stricken was Mr. Bolton, that he remained on the spot where Mr. Halpin had left him, looking after the latter until he arrived at the place where an obstruction had been thrown in his way. By this time, the very breath of Bolton was suspended. Unbounded was his surprise, as he observed Mr. Halpin leap from his horse, swing open the gate, and pass through. Had he seen aright? He rubbed his eyes and looked again. Mr. Halpin had closed the gate, and was on the other side, in the act of mounting his horse.

"Have I done right?" said a voice at this moment.

Bolton started, and, on looking around, saw Mr. Dix.

"Yes, you have done right!" he returned, with an emotion that he could not conceal: "and from my heart I thank you for this kind office. You have saved me from the consequences of a hasty, ill-judged, ill-natured act—consequences that would have been most painful. Oblige me still further Mr. Dix, by letting this matter remain with yourself, at least for the present. Before it comes to the ears of Mr. Halpin, I wish to let him see some better points in my character."

To this, Mr. Dix pledged himself. After repeating his thanks, Mr. Bolton rode away a wiser and a better man.

When Mr. Halpin, some weeks afterwards, made reference to the right of way across Mr. Bolton's land, and asked if he would not sell him a narrow strip on the south edge of his farm, to be fenced off for a road, the latter said—

"No, Mr. Halpin, I will not *sell* you the land; but as it is of little or no value to me, I will cheerfully vacate it for a road, if you are willing to run the fence."

And thus was settled, most amicably, a matter that bid fair, in the beginning, to result in a long and angry disputation, involving loss of money, time, and friendly relationships. Ever after, when disposed to act from a first angry impulse, Mr. Bolton's thoughts would turn to this right-of-way question, and he would become cool and rational in a moment.

COALS OF FIRE.

"I AM sorry, Mr. Grasper, that you should have felt it necessary to proceed to extremities against me," said a care-worn, anxious-looking man, as he entered the store of a thrifty dealer in tapes, needles, and sundry small wares, drawing aside, as he spoke, the personage he addressed. "There was no need of this."

"There's where you and I differ, Mr. Layton," replied Grasper, rudely. "The account has been standing nearly a year, and I have dunned you for it until I am sick and tired."

"I know you have waited a long time for your money," returned the debtor, humbly, "but not, I assure you, because I felt indifferent about paying the bill. I am most anxious to settle it, and would do so this hour, if I had the ability."

"I can't lie out of my money in this way, Mr. Layton. If everybody kept me out of my just dues as long as you have, where do you think I would be? Not in this store, doing as good a business as any one in the street, (Grasper drew himself up with an air of consequence,) but coming out at the little end of the horn, as some of my neighbours are. *I* pay every man his just dues, and it is but right that every man should pay me."

"Where there is a willingness, without present ability, some allowances should be made."

"Humph! I consider a willingness to pay me my own, a very poor substitute for the money."

There was an insulting rudeness in the way Grasper uttered this last sentence, that made the honest blood boil in the veins of his unfortunate debtor. He was tempted to utter a keen rebuke in reply, but restrained himself, and simply made answer:

"Good intentions, I know, are not money. Still, they should be considered as some extenuation in a debtor, and at least exempt him from unnecessarily harsh treatment. No man can tell how it may be with him in the course of a few years, and that, if nothing else, should make every one as lenient towards the unfortunate as possible."

"If you mean to insinuate by that," replied Grasper, in a quick voice, "that I am likely to be in your situation in a few years, I must beg leave to say that I consider your remarks as little better than an insult. It's enough, let me tell you, for you to owe me and not pay me, without coming into my store to insult me. If you have nothing better to say, I see no use in our talking any longer." And Grasper made a motion to turn from his debtor. But the case of Layton was too urgent to let him act as his indignant feelings prompted.

"I meant no offence, I assure you, Mr. Grasper," he said, earnestly,— "I only urged one among many reasons that I could urge, why you should spare a man in my situation."

"While I have as many to urge why I shall not spare you," was angrily retorted. "Your account is sued out, and must take its course, unless you can pay it, or give the required security under the law."

"Won't you take my notes at three, six, nine, and twelve months, for the whole amount I owe you? I am very confident that I can pay you in that time; if not, you may take any steps you please, and I will not say a single word."

"Yes, if you will give me a good endorser."

Layton sighed, and stood silent for some time.

"Will that suit you?" said Grasper.

"I am afraid not. I have never asked for an endorser in my life, and do not know any one who would be willing to go on my paper."

"Well, just as you like. I shall not give up the certainty of a present legal process, for bits of paper with your name on them, you may depend upon it."

The poor debtor sighed again, and more heavily than before.

"If you go on with your suit against me, Mr. Grasper, you will entirely break me up," said he, anxiously.

"That's your look-out, not mine. I want nothing but justice—what the law gives to every man. You have property enough to pay my claim; the law will adjudge it to me, and I will take it. Have you any right to complain?"

"Others will have, if I have not. If you seize upon my goods, and force a sale of them for one-fourth of what they are worth, you injure the interests of my other creditors. They have rights, as well as yourself."

"Let them look after them, then, as I am looking after mine. It is as much as I can do to see to my own interests. But it's no use for you to talk. If you can pay the money or give security, well—if I not, things will have to take their course."

"On this you are resolved?"

"I am."

"Even with the certainty of entirely breaking me up?"

"That, I have before told you, is your own look-out, not mine."

"All I have to say, then, is," remarked Layton, as he turned away, "that I sincerely hope you may, never be placed in my situation; or, if so unfortunate, that you may have a more humane man to deal with than I have."

"Thank you!" was cuttingly replied, "but you needn't waste sympathy on me in advance. I never expect to be in your position. I would sell the shirt off of my back before I would allow a man to ask me for a dollar justly his due, without promptly paying him."

Finding that all his appeals were in vain, Layton retired from the store of his unfeeling creditor. It was too late, now, to make a confession of judgment to some other creditor, who would save, by an amicable sale, the property from sacrifice, and thus secure it for the benefit of all. Grasper had already obtained a judgment and taken out an execution, under which a levy had been made by the sheriff, and a sale was ordered to take place in a week. Nothing could now hinder the onward progress of affairs to a disastrous crisis, but the payment of the debt, or its security. As neither the one nor the other was possible, the sale was advertised, the store of Layton closed, and the sacrifice made. Goods that cost four times the amount of Grasper's claim were sold for just enough to cover it, and the residue of the stock left for the other creditors. These were immediately called together, and all that the ruined debtor possessed in the world given up to them.

"Take my furniture and all," said he. "Even after that is added to this poor remnant, your claims will be very far from satisfied. Had I dreamed that Grasper was so selfish a man as to disregard every one's interests in the eager pursuit of his own, I would, long before he had me in his power, have made a general assignment for the benefit of the whole. But it is too late now for regrets; they avail nothing. I still have health, and an unbroken spirit. I am ready to try again, and, it may be, that success will crown my efforts. If so, you have the pledge of an honest man, that every dollar of present deficit shall be made up. Can I say more?"

Fortunately for Layton, there was no Grasper among the unsatisfied portion of his creditors. He was pitied more than censured. Every man said "no" to the proposition to surrender up his household furniture.

"Let that remain untouched. We will not visit your misfortunes upon your family."

After all his goods had been sold off to the best advantage, a little over sixty cents on the dollar was paid. The loss to all parties would have been light, had Grasper not sacrificed so much to secure his own debt.

Regarding Layton as an honest man, and pitying his condition, with a large family on his hands to provide for, a few of his creditors had a conference on the subject of his affairs, which resulted in a determination to make an effort to put him on his feet again. The first thing done was to get all parties to sign a permanent release of obligations still held against him, thus making him free from all legal responsibilities for past transactions. The next thing was to furnish him with a small, saleable stock of goods, on a liberal credit.

On this basis, Layton started again in the world, with a confident spirit. The old store was given up, and a new one taken at about half the rent. It so happened, that this store was next to the one occupied by Grasper, who, now that he had got his own, and had been made sensible of the indignation of the other creditors for what he had done, felt rather ashamed to look his neighbour in the face.

"Who has taken your store?" he asked of the owner of the property next to his own, seeing him taking down the bill that had been up for a few days.

"Your old friend Layton," replied the man, who was familiar with the story of Layton's recent failure.

"You are not in earnest?" said Grasper, looking serious.

"Yes—I have rented it to Layton."

"He has just been broken up root and branch, and can't get credit for a dollar. How can he go into business?"

"Some friends have assisted him."

"Indeed! I didn't suppose a man in his condition had many friends."

"Oh, yes. An honest man always has friends. Layton is an honest man, and I would trust him now as freely as before. He has learned wisdom by experience, and, if ever he gets into difficulties again, will take good care that no one man gets an undue preference over another. His recent failure, I am told, was caused by one of his creditors, who, in the eager desire to get his own, sacrificed a large amount of property, to the injury of the other creditors."

Grasper did not venture to make any reply to this, lest he should betray, by his manner, the fact that he was the individual to whom allusion was made. He need not have been careful on this point, as the person with whom he was conversing knew very well who was the grasping creditor.

A day or two afterwards, Layton took possession of his new store, and commenced arranging his goods. Grasper felt uneasy when he saw the doors and windows open, and the goods arriving. He did not wish to meet Layton. But this could not now be avoided. Much as he loved money, and much as he had congratulated himself for the promptness by which he had secured his debt, he now more than half wished that he had been less stringent in his proceedings.

It was the custom of Grasper to come frequently to his door, and stand with his thumbs in the arm-holes of his waistcoat, and look forth with a self-satisfied air. But not once did he venture thus to stand upon his own threshold on the day Layton commenced receiving his goods. When business called him out, he was careful to step into the street, so much turned away from the adjoining store, that he could not see the face of any one who might be standing in the entrance. On returning, he would glide along close to the houses, and enter quickly his own door. By this carefulness to avoid meeting his old debtor, Grasper managed not to come into direct contact with him for some time. But this was not always to be the case. One day, just as he was about entering his store, Layton came out of his own door, and they met face to face.

"Ah! How are you, friend Layton?" he said, with an air of forced cordiality, extending his hand as he spoke. "So you have become my next-door neighbour?"

"Yes," was the quiet reply, made in a pleasant manner, and without the least appearance of resentment for the past.

"I am really glad to find you are on your feet again," said Grasper, affecting an interest which he did not feel. "For the misfortunes you have suffered, I always felt grieved, although, perhaps, I was a little to blame for hastening the crisis in your affairs. But I had waited a long time for my money, you know."

"Yes, and others will now have to wait a great deal longer, in consequence of your hasty action," replied Layton, speaking seriously, but not in a way to offend.

"I am very sorry, but it can't be helped now," said Grasper, looking a little confused. "I only took the ordinary method of securing my own. If I had not taken care of myself, somebody would have come in and swept the whole. You know you couldn't possibly have stood it much longer."

"If you think it right, Mr. Grasper, I have nothing now to say," returned Layton.

"You certainly could not call it wrong for a man to sue another who has the means, and yet refuses to pay what he owes him?"

"I think it wrong, Mr. Grasper," replied Layton, "for any man to injure others in his over-eagerness to get his own, and this you did. You seized four, times as many goods as would have paid your claim if they had been fairly sold, and had them sacrificed for one-fourth of their value, thus wronging my other creditors out of some three thousand dollars in the present, and taxing my future efforts to make good what was no better than thrown into the sea. You had no moral right to do this, although you had the power. This is my opinion of the matter, Mr. Grasper; and I freely express it, in the hope that, if ever another man is so unfortunate as to get in your debt without the means of present payment, that you will be less exacting with him than you were with me."

Grasper writhed in spirit under this cutting rebuke of Layton, which was given seriously, but not in anger. He tried to make a great many excuses, to none of which Layton made any reply. He had said all he wished to say on the subject. After this, the two met frequently—more frequently than Grasper cared about meeting the man he had injured. Several times he alluded, indirectly, to the past, in an apologetic way, but Layton never appeared to understand the allusion. This was worse to Grasper than if he had come out and said over and over again just what he thought of the other's conduct.

Five years from the day Layton commenced business anew, he made his last dividend upon the deficit that stood against him at the time his creditors generously released him and set him once more upon his feet. He was doing a very good business, and had a credit much more extensive than he cared about using. No one was more ready to sell him than Grasper, who frequently importuned him to make bills at his store. This he sometimes did, but made it a point never to give his note for the purchase, always paying the cash and receiving a discount.

"I'd as lief have your note as your money," Grasper would sometimes say.

"I always prefer paying the cash while I have it," was generally the answer. "In this way, I make a double profit on my sales."

The true reason why he would not give his note to Grasper, was his determination never to be in debt to any man who, in an extremity, would oppress him. This reason was more than suspected by Grasper and it worried him exceedingly. If Layton had refused to buy from him at all, he would have felt less annoyance.

Year after year passed on, and Layton's business gradually enlarged, until he was doing at least four times as much as Grasper, who now found himself much oftener the buyer from, than the seller to, Layton. At first, in making bills with Layton, he always made it a point to cash them. But this soon became inconvenient, and he was forced to say, in making a pretty heavy purchase—

"I shall have to give my note for this."

"Just as you please, Mr. Grasper, it is all the same to me," replied Layton, indifferently. "I had as lief have your note as your money."

Grasper felt his cheek burn. For the hundredth time, he repented of one act in his life.

A few months after this, Grasper found himself very hard pressed to meet his payments. He had been on the borrowing list for a good while, and had drawn so often and so largely upon business friends, that he had almost worn out his welcome. For one of his heavy days he had been endeavouring to make provision in advance, but had not succeeded in obtaining all the money needed, when the day arrived. In his extremity, and as a last resort, yet with a most heart-sinking reluctance, he called in to see Layton.

"Have you seven hundred dollars more than you want to-day?" he asked, in a tone that betrayed his unwillingness to ask the favour, although he strove to appear indifferent.

"I have, and it's at your service," was promptly and cheerfully replied. "Shall I fill you a check?"

"If you please," said Grasper; "I have a very heavy payment to make to-day, and find money tighter than usual. When do you with me to return it to you?" he asked, as he took the check.

"Oh! in three or four days. Will that do?"

"It will suit me exactly. I am very much obliged to you, indeed."

"You are very welcome. I shall always be happy to accommodate you in a similar way. I generally have something over."

When Grasper returned to his own store, his cheek burned, his heart beat quicker, and his breathing was oppressed. He felt humbled in his own eyes. To the man whom he once so cruelly wronged he had been compelled to go for a favour, and that man had generously returned him good for evil.

He was unhappy until he could replace the money he had borrowed, which was in a day or two, and even then he still felt very uncomfortable.

After this, Grasper of course was frequently driven to the necessity of getting temporary loans from Layton, which were always made in a way which showed that it gave his neighbour real pleasure to accommodate him.

Gradually, difficulties gathered around Grasper so thickly, that he found it almost impossible to keep his head above water. Two thirds of his time were spent in efforts to raise money to meet his payments, and the other third in brooding sadly and inactively over the embarrassed condition of his affairs. This being the case, his business suffered inevitably. Instead of going on and making handsome profits, as he had once done, he was actually losing money, and that, too, rapidly; for, when he bought, he often made imprudent purchases, and when he sold, he made three bad debts where he formerly made one.

At last, a crisis came in his affairs, as come it must, sooner or later, under such a system. A stoppage and ruin he saw to be inevitable. He owed more borrowed money than he could possibly return within the time for which he had obtained it, and had, besides, large payments to make in bank within the period. Any effort to get through, he saw would be hopeless, and he determined to give up; not, however, without securing something for himself.

"Twenty cents less in the dollar for my creditors," he argued, "will not kill them, and that difference will be quite important to me. When the storm blows over, it will give me the means of hoisting sail again."

At this time, Grasper owed Layton two thousand dollars borrowed money, and two thousand dollars in notes of hand, given for goods purchased of him.

"It won't do," he said to himself, "to let *him* lose any thing. I should never be able to look him in the face again, after what has happened between us. No—no—I must see *him* safe."

On the next day, Grasper called in to see Layton. His face was serious.

"Can I say a word to you alone?" he asked.

"Certainly," and the two men retired to a private part of the store. Grasper had never felt so wretched in all his life. After two or three efforts to speak, he at last found voice enough to say—

"Mr. Layton, I have very bad news to tell you. It is impossible for me to go on any longer. I shall stop to-morrow, inevitably. I owe you two thousand dollars in borrowed money and two thousand in notes, making, in all, four thousand dollars. I don't wish *you* to lose any thing by me, and, to secure your borrowed money, I have brought you good notes for two thousand dollars, which is the best I can possibly do. For the other two thousand dollars, I want you to come into my store, and take your choice of any thing there, which I will sell you, and take my own notes back in payment. That is the best I can possibly do for you, Mr. Layton, and it will be far better, I fear, than I shall be able to do for any one else."

Layton was taken entirely by surprise.

"What you say astonishes me, Mr. Grasper; I thought you were doing a very flourishing business?"

"And so I would have been, had I not ventured a little beyond my depth, and got cramped for money to meet my payments. A neglect of my business was the inevitable consequence; for, when all my time was taken up in raising money, I had none left to see after my business in a proper manner. Bad debts have been one of the consequences, and profitless operations another, until I am involved beyond the power of extrication, and must see every thing fall in ruins about my head."

"It really grieves me to hear you say this," replied Layton, not offering to take the notes which Grasper was still holding out for his acceptance. "But, perhaps, you magnify your difficulties. Don't you think some temporary relief would help you over your present embarrassments?"

"No: nothing temporary would be of any avail."

"Have you any objection to letting me see a full statement of your affairs? Perhaps I can suggest something better than a failure, which is almost always the very worst thing that can be done."

"Most gladly will I do so, Mr. Layton," returned Grasper; "and if you can point out any way by which I can get over my present difficulties, I shall be for ever under obligation to you."

An examination into Grasper's business satisfied Layton that a few thousand dollars would save it.

"You need not fail," he said, cheerfully, to the unhappy man, as soon as he fully comprehended the state of his affairs.

"What is to prevent it?" eagerly asked the embarrassed merchant.

"You want more money," said Layton.

"I know that. Seven or eight thousand dollars would relieve me, if I had the use of it for one or two years, so that I could devote all my time to business. I have enough to do. All that is wanted is to do it well."

"Yes, I see that clearly enough."

"But the money, where is that to come from?"

"It can be raised, I think. In fact, if you will secure me against loss, I will take your notes and raise it for you."

"I will secure you upon every thing that I possess," was instantly replied.

"Very well. That will do. How much money must you have to-morrow?"

"Two thousand dollars."

"That can be managed easily enough. I will see that it is raised. In the mean time, get all arrangements for the security in progress, so that I can take your notes and pass them through bank as fast as you need to have money."

Grasper was overpowered. He could hardly believe that he heard aright. This was the man who had been driven by his grasping spirit into bankruptcy, and utterly ruined. The thought again flashed through his mind, and sent the blood burning to his face. Pride for a moment tempted him to refuse the offered kindness; but there was too much at stake—he could not do it. While the act of Layton heaped coals of fire upon his head, he had no alternative but to submit to a thing only less painful than utter ruin. From ruin he was saved; but he was an altered and an humbled man. Many times since have unfortunate debtors been in his power, and, although he has not acted towards them with much liberality, (for it was not in him to do so,) he has not oppressed them.

A NEW PLEASURE.

THE whole purpose of Mr. Bolton's life had been the accumulation of property, with an end to his own gratification. To part with a dollar was therefore ever felt as the giving up of a prospective good; and it acted as the abridgment of present happiness. Appeals to Mr. Bolton's benevolence had never been very successful; and, in giving, he had not experienced the blessing which belongs of right to good deeds. The absolute selfishness of his feelings wronged him of what was justly his due.

Thus passed the life of Mr. Bolton. Dollar was added to dollar, house to house, and field to field. Yet he was never satisfied with gaining; for the little he had, looked so small compared with the wealth of the world, after the whole of which his heart really panted, as to appear at times actually insignificant. Thus, as he grew older, he set a value upon what he had, as the means of gaining more, and in his parting with money, did so at the expense of a daily increasing reluctance.

In the beginning of life, Mr. Bolton possessed a few generous feelings, the remains of early and innocent states stored up in childhood. His mother, a true woman, perceiving the strong selfish and accumulative bent of his character, had sought in every possible way to implant in his mind feelings of benevolence and regard for others. One mode of doing this had been to introduce him into scenes that appealed to his sympathies. She often took him with her to see poor or sick persons, and so interested him in them as to create a desire in his mind to afford relief. So soon as she perceived this desire awakened, she devised some mode of bringing it into activity, so that he might feel the delights which spring from a consciousness of having done good to another.

But so strong was the lad's hereditary love of self, that she ever found difficulty in inducing him to sacrifice what he already considered his own, in the effort to procure blessings for others, no matter how greatly they stood in need. If urged to spend a sixpence of his own for such a purpose, he would generally reply:

"But you've got a great many more sixpences than I have, mother: why don't you spend them?"

To this, Mrs. Bolton would answer as appropriately as possible; but she found but poor success in her efforts, which were never relaxed.

In early manhood, as Mr. Bolton began to come in actual contact with the world, the remains of early states of innocence and sympathy with others came back, as we have intimated, upon him, and he acted, in many instances, with a generous disregard of self. But as he bent his mind more and more earnestly to the accumulation of money, these feelings had less and less influence over him. And as dollar after dollar was added to his store, his interest in the welfare of others grew less and less active. Early friendships were gradually forgotten, and the first natural desire to see early friends prosperous like himself, gradually died out. "Every man for himself," became the leading principle of his life; and he acted upon it on all occasions. In taking a pew in church and regularly attending worship every Sabbath, he was governed by the idea that it was respectable to do so, and gave a man a standing in society, that reacted favourably upon his worldly interests. In putting his name to a subscription paper, a thing not always to be avoided, even by him, a business view of the matter was invariably taken, and the satisfaction of mind experienced on the occasion arose from the reflection that the act would benefit him in the long run. As to the minor charities, in the doing of which the left hand has no acquaintance with the deeds of the right hand, Mr. Bolton never indulged in them. If his left hand had known the doings of his right hand in matters of this kind, said hand would not have been much wiser for the knowledge.

Thus life went on; and Mr. Bolton was ever busy in gathering in his golden harvest; so busy, that he had no time for any thing else, not even to enjoy what he possessed. At last, he was sixty years old, and his wealth extended to many hundreds of thousands of dollars. But he was farther from being satisfied than ever, and less happy than at any former period in his life.

One cause of unhappiness arose from the fact that, as a rich man, he was constantly annoyed with applications to do a rich man's part in the charities of the day. And to these applications it was impossible always to turn a deaf ear. Give he must sometimes, and giving always left a pain behind, because the gift came not from a spirit of benevolence. There were other and various causes of unhappiness, all of which combining, made Mr. Bolton, as old age came stealing upon him, about as miserable as a man could well be. Money, in his eyes the greatest good, had not brought the peace of mind to which he had looked forward, and the days came and went without a smile. His children had grown up and passed into the world, and were, as he had been at their ages, so all-absorbed by the love of gain, as to have little love to spare for any thing else.

About this time, Mr. Bolton, having made one or two losing operations, determined to retire from business, invest all his money in real estate and other securities, and let the management of these investments constitute his future employment. In this new occupation he found so little to do in comparison with his former busy life, that the change proved adverse, so far as his repose of mind was concerned.

It happened, about this time, that Mr. Bolton had occasion to go some twenty miles into the country. On returning home, and when within a few miles of the city, his carriage was overset, and he had the misfortune to fracture a limb. This occurred near a pleasant little farm-house that stood a few hundred yards from the road; the owner of which, seeing the accident, ran to the overturned carriage and assisted to extricate the injured man. Seeing how badly he was hurt, he had him removed to his house, and then, taking a horse, rode off two miles for a physician. In the mean time, the driver of Mr. Bolton's carriage was despatched to the city for some of his family and his own physician. The country doctor and the one from the city arrived about the same time. On making a careful examination as to the nature of Mr. Bolton's injuries, it was found that his right leg, above the knee, was broken, and that one of his ankles was dislocated. He was suffering great pain, and was much exhausted. As quickly as it could be done, the bone was set, and the dislocation reduced. By this time it was nightfall, and too late to think seriously of returning home before morning. The moment Mr. Gray, the farmer, saw the thoughts of the injured man and his friends directed towards the city, he promptly invited them to remain in his house all night, and as much longer as the nature of Mr. Bolton's injuries might require. This invitation was thankfully accepted.

During the night, Mr. Bolton suffered a great deal of pain, and in the morning, when the physicians arrived, it was found that his injured limb was much inflamed. Of course, a removal to the city was out of the question. The doctors declared that the attempt would be made at the risk of his life. Farmer Gray said that such a thing must not be thought of until the patient was fully able to bear the journey; and the farmer's wife as earnestly remonstrated against any attempt at having the injured man disturbed until it could be perfectly safe to do so. Both tendered the hospitalities of their humble home with so much sincerity, that Mr. Bolton felt that he could accept of them with perfect freedom.

It was a whole month ere the old gentleman was in a condition to bear the journey to town; and not once in the whole of that time had Mr. and Mrs. Gray seemed weary of his presence, nor once relaxed in their efforts to make him comfortable. As Mr. Bolton was about leaving, he tendered the farmer, with many expressions of gratitude for the kindness he had received, a hundred-dollar bill, as some small compensation for the trouble and expense he had occasioned him and his family. But Mr. Gray declined the offer, saying, as he did so:

"I have only done what common humanity required, Mr. Bolton; and were I to receive money, all the pleasure I now experience would be gone."

It was in vain that Mr. Bolton urged the farmer's acceptance of some remuneration. Mr. Gray was firm in declining to the last. All that could be done was to send Mrs. Gray a handsome present from the city; but this did not entirely relieve the mind of Mr. Bolton from the sense of obligation under which the disinterested kindness of the farmer had laid him; and thoughts of this tended to soften his feelings, and to awaken, in a small measure, the human sympathies which had so long slumbered in his bosom.

Several months passed before Mr. Bolton was able to go out, and then he resumed his old employment of looking after his rents, and seeking for new and safe investments that promised some better returns than he was yet receiving.

One day, a broker, who was in the habit of doing business for Mr. Bolton, said to him:

"If you want to buy a small, well-cultivated farm, at about half what it is worth, I think I know where you can get one."

"Do you?"

"Yes. Three years ago it was bought for three thousand dollars, and seven hundred paid down in cash. Only eight hundred dollars have since been paid on it; and as the time for which the mortgage was to remain has now expired, a foreclosure is about to take place. By a little management, I am satisfied that I can get you the farm for the balance due on the mortgage."

"That is, for fifteen hundred dollars?"

"Yes."

"Is the farm worth that? Will it be a good investment?"

"It is in the highest state of cultivation. The owner has spent too much money upon it. This, with the loss of his entire crop of wheat, rye, corn, oats, and hay, last year, has crippled him, and made it impossible to pay off the mortgage."

"How came he to meet with this loss?"

"His barn was struck by lightning."

"That was unfortunate."

"The farm will command, at the lowest, two hundred and fifty dollars rent; and by forcing a sale just at this time, it can be had for fifteen hundred or two thousand dollars—half its real value."

"It would be a good investment at that."

"Capital. I would advise you to secure it."

After making some brief inquiries as to its location, the quality of the land, the improvements, etc., Mr. Bolton told the broker, in whom he had great confidence, that he might buy the property for him, if he could obtain it for any thing below two thousand dollars. This the broker said he could easily do, as the business of foreclosure was in his own hands.

In due time, Mr. Bolton was informed by his agent in the matter, that a sale under the mortgage had taken place, and that, by means of the little management proposed, he had succeeded in keeping away all competition in bidding. The land, stock, farming implements, and all, had been knocked down at a price that just covered the encumbrance on the estate, and were the property of Mr. Bolton, at half their real value.

"That was a good speculation," said the gray-headed money-lover, when his agent informed him of what he had been doing.

"First-rate," replied the broker. "The farm is worth every cent of three thousand dollars. Poor Gray! I can't help feeling sorry for him. But it's his luck. He valued his farm at three thousand five hundred dollars. A week ago he counted himself worth two thousand dollars, clean. Now he isn't worth a copper. Fifteen hundred dollars and three or four years' labour thrown away into the bargain. But it's his luck! So the world goes. He must try again. It will all go in his lifetime."

"Gray? Is that the man's name?" inquired Mr. Bolton. His voice was changed.

"Yes. I thought I had mentioned his name."

"I didn't remark it, if you did. It's the farm adjoining Harvey's, on the north?"

"Yes."

"I have had it in my mind, all along, that it was the one on the south."

"No."

"When did you see Mr. Gray?"

"He was here about half an hour ago."

"How does he feel about the matter?"

"He takes it hard, of course. Any man would. But it's his luck, and he must submit. It's no use crying over disappointments and losses, in this world."

Mr. Bolton mused for a long time.

"I'll see you again to-morrow," he said, at length. "Let every thing remain as it is until then."

The man who had been for so many years sold, as it were, to selfishness, found himself checked at last by the thought of another. While just in the act of grasping a money advantage, the interest of another arose up, and made him pause.

"If it had been any one else," said he to himself, as he walked slowly homeward, "all would have been plain sailing. But—but"—

The sentence was not finished.

"It won't do to turn HIM away," was at length uttered. "He shall have the farm at a very moderate rent."

Still, these concessions of selfishness did not relieve the mind of Mr. Bolton, nor make him feel more willing to meet the man who had done him so groat a kindness, and in such a disinterested spirit.

All that day, and for a portion of the night that followed, Mr. Bolton continued to think over the difficulty in which he found himself placed; and the more he thought, the less willing did he feel to take the great advantage of the poor farmer at first contemplated. After falling asleep, his mind continued occupied with the same subject, and in the dreams that came to him, he lived over a portion of the past.

He was again a helpless invalid, and the kind farmer and his excellent wife were ministering, as before, to his comfort. His heart was full of grateful feelings. Then a change came suddenly. He stood the spectator of a widely-spread ruin which had fallen upon the excellent Mr. Gray and his family. A fierce tempest was sweeping over his fields, and levelling all-houses, trees, and grain—in ruin to the earth. A word spoken by him would have saved all; he felt this: but he did not speak the word. The look of reproach suddenly cast upon him by the farmer so stung him that he awoke; and from that time until the day dawned, he lay pondering on the course of conduct he had best pursue.

The advantage of the purchase he had made was so great, that Mr. Bolton thought of relinquishing it with great reluctance. On the other hand, his obligation to the farmer was of such a nature, that he must, in clinging to his bargain, forfeit his self-respect, and must suffer a keen sense of mortification, if not dishonour, at any time that he happened to meet Mr. Gray face to face. Finally, after a long struggle, continued through several days, he resolved to forego the good he had attempted to grasp.

How many years since this man had done a generous action! since he had relinquished a selfish and sordid purpose out of regard to another's well-being! And now it had cost him a desperate struggle; but after the trial was past, his mind became tranquil, and he could think of what he was about to do with an emotion of pleasure that was new in his experience. Immediately on this resolution being formed, Mr. Bolton called upon his agent. His first inquiry was:

"When did you see Gray?"

"The previous owner of your farm?"

"Yes."

"Not since the sale. You told me to let every thing remain as it was."

"Hasn't he called?"

"No."

"The loss of his farm must be felt as a great misfortune."

"No doubt of that. Every man feels his losses as misfortunes. But we all have to take the good and the bad in life together. It's his luck, and he must put up with it."

"I wonder if he hasn't other property?"

"No."

"Are you certain?"

"Oh, yes. I know exactly what he was worth. He had been overseer for Elbertson for several years, and while there, managed to save seven hundred dollars, with which he paid down the cash required in purchasing his farm. Since then, he has been paying off the mortgage that remained on the property, and but for the burning of his barn, might have prevented a result that has been so disastrous to himself. But it's an ill wind that blows nobody any good. In every loss, somebody gains; and the turn of the die has been in your favour this time."

Mr. Bolton did not appear to feel as much satisfaction at this view of the case as the broker anticipated; and seeing this, he changed the subject, by asking some question about the consummation of the sale under the mortgage.

"I'll see you about that to-morrow," said Mr. Bolton.

"Very well," was replied.

After some more conversation, Mr. Bolton left the office of his agent.

For years, farmer Gray had been toiling late and early, to become the full owner of his beautiful farm. Its value had much increased since it had come into his possession, and he looked forward with pleasure to the time when it would be his own beyond all doubt. But the loss of an entire year's crop, through the burning of his barn, deeply tried and dispirited him. From this grievous disappointment, his spirits were beginning to rise, when the sudden foreclosure of the mortgage and hurried sale of his farm crushed all his hopes to the earth.

Who the real purchaser of his farm was, Mr. Gray did not know, for the broker had bought in his own name. So bewildered was the farmer by the suddenly-occurring disaster, that, for several days subsequent to the sale, he remained almost totally paralyzed in mind. No plans were laid for the future, nor even those ordinary steps for the present taken, that common prudence would suggest; he wandered about the farm, or sat at home, dreamily musing upon what seemed the utter ruin of all his best hopes in life. While in this state, he was surprised by a visit from Mr. Bolton. The old gentleman, in taking him by the hand, said—"What's the matter, my friend? You appear in trouble."

"And I am in trouble," was unhesitatingly answered.

"Not so deep but that you may get out of it again, I hope?"

Mr. Gray shook his head in a desponding way.

"What *is* the trouble?" Mr. Bolton inquired.

"I have lost my farm."

"Oh, no!"

"It is too true; it has been sold for a mortgage of fifteen hundred dollars. Though I have already paid more than that sum on account of the purchase, it only brought enough to pay the encumbrance, and I am ruined."

The farmer was deeply disturbed, and Mr. Bolton's feelings were much interested.

"Don't be so troubled, my good friend," said the old gentleman. "You rendered me a service in the time of need, and it is now in my power to return it. The farm is still yours. I hold the mortgage, and you need not fear another foreclosure."

Some moments passed after this announcement before Mr. Gray's mind became clear, and his entire self-possession returned; then grasping the hand of Mr. Bolton, he thanked him with all the eloquence a grateful heart inspires. It was the happiest moment the old merchant had seen for years. The mere possession of a thousand or two of dollars seemed as nothing to the pleasure he felt at having performed a good action; or, rather, at having refrained from doing an evil one.

As he rode back to the city, reflecting upon what he had done, and recalling the delight shown by Mr. Gray and his kind partner, who had attended him so carefully while he lay a sufferer beneath their roof, his heart swelled in his bosom with a new and happy emotion.

Having once permitted himself to regard another with an unselfish interest, that interest continued; it seemed as if he could not do enough for the farmer in the way of aiding him to develop the resources of his little property. In this he did not merely stop at suggestions, but tendered something more substantial and available. Nor did the feelings awakened in his mind run all in this direction; occasions enough offered for him to be generous to others, and to refrain from oppression for the sake of gain. Many of these were embraced, and Mr. Bolton, in realizing the fact that it is sometimes more blessed to give than to receive, found in the latter years of his life a NEW PLEASURE—the pleasure of benevolence.

THE DAUGHTER-IN-LAW.

"I SHALL love your mother very much, Charles, but do you think she will love me?" said a graceful young creature, leaning with an air of tender confidence upon the arm of her companion, and looking earnestly in his face. She was a little above the ordinary stature, with a form so delicate as to appear almost fragile, a pure semi-transparent skin, and a cheek—

> "Like the apple-tree blossom,
> By the dew-fountain fed,
> Was the bloom of her cheek,
> With its white and its red."

Eyes of heaven's own blue beamed with love and delight, as they wandered over the frank, honest face of the young man, who stood looking down into them, as they reflected back his own image. He could not love himself without harm to himself, but he could gaze on, and love to gaze for ever upon the image of himself pictured in those dear eyes, and yet be innocent.

"Love you, Ellen? How can she help loving you?"

"I do not know why any one should love me," was the artless reply.

"I do not know how any one can help loving you."

"Ah, you may think so, but every one does not see with your eyes; and maybe, you are only blinded. I am not perfect, Charles; don't forget that."

"You are perfect to me, and that is all I ask. But say, Ellen, dear, sha'n't we be married in a month?"

"I am so young, Charles; and then I ought to be certain that your mother is willing. Does she know all about it? You have written to her, have you not?"

The young man did not reply for some moments. Then he said— "Never fear, Ellen; my mother will love you as her own child, when she sees and knows you. I have not written about you to her, because, as I must tell you, my mother, though one of the best of women, is a little proud of her standing in society. The moment I write to her on the subject, she will have a dozen grave questions to ask about your family, and whether they are connected with this great personage or that—questions that I despair of answering, in a letter, to her satisfaction. But your dear face will explain all, and stop all inquiries, when I present you to her as my wife."

"Don't be so certain of that, Charles. If your mother is proud of her family, she will be mortified and displeased should her son marry an unknown girl."

"The proudest mother on earth would receive you into her bosom, and call you daughter, without an emotion of wounded pride," was the lover's confident reply. "I know it. I know my mother too well, not to be confident on this subject."

"You ought to know, Charles; but I would much rather be certain. I love you better than my life; but if I thought that your marrying me would separate you from your mother's love, I would never consent to a union. Ah, there can be no love so pure, so deep, so unselfish as a mother's love. A mother! Oh, how sweet the name! how holy the office! I can remember, though but faintly, my own mother. I was but a little girl when I lost her, but I still see her face as it often bent over me while I lay in my bed, and still, at times, can hear her voice. Oh, what would I not have given had she lived! Ah, Charles, be sure that in no act of your life you wrong your mother, or give her pain."

Charles Linden belonged to a family that claimed descent from some distinguished ancestor on the mother's side—some one who had come from England a long time ago, and who, when there, was ranked one of gentle blood. Of the worth of his principles, little was known. He may have been a high-minded and honourable man, or he may have possessed qualities worthy of the detestation of all. Be that as it may, Mrs. Linden valued herself highly on having come down in a right line, through three generations, from this distinguished individual; and there were plenty to estimate her by her own standard. As a woman, taking her for what she was worth, she would have done very well, and received from all sensible people due consideration; but her true character as a woman was glossed over and somewhat defaced by her pride. She did not regard her own qualities of mind as any thing—her standing as one of the true aristocrats of society was every thing. As for her husband, little was ever said about his ancestors; he had no scruples, while living, of an investigation, for he feared none. His father was a wealthy merchant, and his grandfather an honest farmer, who fought for his country during the whole revolutionary campaign. The old soldier left to his son the inheritance of sound moral principles, a good education, and an enthusiastic love of his country. With these as his only patrimony, he started in the world. At the age of fifty, he died, leaving to his children an untarnished name and forty thousand dollars a piece.

The father of Charles Linden had been in business several years when this event took place, and had already acquired by his own exertions, as well as by marriage, a handsome property. He died when Charles, his eldest son, was but sixteen, leaving three children, two sons and one daughter; and a widow estimated to be worth a hundred thousand dollars. To each of the children he left fifty thousand dollars. This did not please the aristocratic notions of the mother. It would have been more in consonance with her views, if but one-third of the whole property had been left to her, and the balance to their eldest son, with the reservation of small annuities for the other children. In her own mind she determined to will all she had to Charles, with the distinct proviso that he took possession of it only on the condition of dropping his father's name, and assuming that of her family, which was Beauchamp.

Long before he was twenty-one years of age, she commenced her insidious attacks upon his native manliness of character, which showed itself in a disposition to value every thing with which he came in contact, according to intrinsic worth. He never bought of the family of any one with whom he was brown into association, but of qualities of head and heart. At school he had learned how to estimate individual worth; books, truly American books, conceived by American minds, strengthened the right impression so made. When, therefore, Mrs. Linden attempted to show him that family was the primary thing to be considered in his associations with people, her efforts were altogether fruitless.

All persons of Mrs. Linden's way of thinking make it a point to take the marriage of their children pretty much into their own hands, believing that their external views on the subject are far better than the internal attraction toward an object that can be truly loved, which their children imagine they feel—or, as they say, "imagine." The mother of Charles understood well her duty in this matter. Long before her son had passed his fourteenth year, she had made a selection for him in a little Miss, younger than he was by two years, named Antoinette Billings. Antoinette's mother was a woman after Mrs. Linden's own heart. She understood the first distant hint made on the subject, and readily came to a fair and open understanding with Mrs. Linden. Then it was managed so that the children were much together, and they were taught to look upon each other as engaged for marriage at some future day.

Charles was a fine, noble-hearted boy; but Antoinette was a spoiled, pert, selfish creature, and had but little control over her tempers, that were by no means amiable. It was not long before the future husband, so called, wisely determined that Miss Antoinette should never be his wife, and he told his mother so in very plain language. Mrs. Linden tried every art in her power to influence Charles, but it was no use. He inherited too much truly noble blood from this independent, right-thinking father.

At the age of twenty-one, he left his native place and entered into business in a neighbouring city. His mother parted with him reluctantly; but there were strong reasons why he should go, and she did not feel that it would be right to oppose him.

About a year after his removal from P——to his new place of residence, Charles Linden met Ellen Fleetwood. She had come recently from one of the Eastern States, and resided in the family of a distant relative. His first impressions were favourable—each subsequent meeting confirmed them—and, length, he found himself really attached to her. So little of his mother's peculiar spirit had he imbibed, that it did not once occur to him to ask about her family until he had made up his mind to offer himself in marriage. Inquiry on this subject resulted in the discovery that Ellen's parents were distinguished from the mass in no particular way. They had married early, and her mother died early. Her father, whose very existence seemed to have been wrapped up in that of his wife, went away soon after her death, and never returned. It was believed by his friends that he did not survive her long. Ellen was then five years old. An aunt adopted her and raised her as her own child. A year before Linden met her, this aunt had died, leaving her a small income. She removed shortly after this event, at the request of a relative—the only surviving one, as far as she knew—and now lived with her. Of the precise character of the father and mother, he could learn nothing. Ellen, therefore, neither lost nor gained any thing in his eyes by birth. For what she was to him, and for that alone, he loved her—and loved purely and tenderly.

An engagement took place in a few months after their acquaintance commenced. It was shortly afterwards that the conversation detailed in the opening of our story commenced, from which it will appear that Charles had not yet ventured to inform his mother of the choice he had made. Knowing the strength of her peculiar prejudices, he had every thing to fear, as far as opposition was concerned. The fact that Ellen appeared so anxious to obtain her favour made him less willing to risk the consequences of informing his mother that he had made his choice of a wife. He knew she would oppose a marriage most strenuously. What the effect of such opposition upon Ellen would be, it would be impossible to tell;—it might, he feared, lead her to decline his offer. For this reason, he urged an immediate union; and wished it to take place without his parent's knowledge. Ellen opposed this earnestly, but was finally induced to yield. They were married, and started the next morning to visit Mrs. Linden. Two days before, Charles had written to inform his mother of what had taken place, and of his intended return home, on a short visit, with his bride.

"My dear mother," a portion of his letter read, "I know you will be grieved, and, I fear, offended at what I have done; but wait only for a day or two, until you see my Ellen—your Ellen, let me say—and you will be grieved and angry no longer. She will love you as only an unselfish child can love a mother; and you will love her the moment you see her. I have talked to her from the first about you, and she has already so pure an affection for you, that she is longing to see you and throw herself upon your bosom. Oh! let me beg of you to receive her in the spirit with which she is coming to you. Be to her a mother, as she wishes to be to you a child."

It was not without many misgivings at heart that Charles Linden set out to visit his mother. These could not be felt without their effects being perceived by Ellen, who was tremblingly anxious about her reception. Her spirits became in consequence depressed, and more than once Charles found tears stealing from beneath her half-closed eyelids. He understood well the cause, and strove, but vainly, to assure her that all would be as her heart could wish.

It was nearly nightfall when the carriage that conveyed them from the steamboat landing drew up before the elegant residence of Mrs. Linden. Charles hurried in with his bride in a tumult of anxiety. A servant was sent up to announce his arrival. Five minutes passed, and they still sat alone in the parlour—Charles deeply agitated, and Ellen looking pale and frightened.

"What can keep her so long?" the young man had just said, in a husky whisper, when the door opened and his mother entered with a slow, dignified step, her face calm, but severe, and her tall person drawn up to its full height. Charles started forward, but the instantly raised hand and forbidding aspect of his mother restrained him.

"Don't come near me," said she, coldly—"you have done that for which I never shall forgive you. Go at once from my presence, with the mean-spirited creature who has dared to suppose that I would acknowledge as my daughter one who has corrupted and robbed me of my son. Go! We are mother and son no longer. I dissolve the tie. Go!"

And the mother, whose assumed calmness had given way to a highly excited manner, waved her hand imperatively towards the door.

Ellen, who had started up at the moment Mrs. Linden appeared, now came forward, and, throwing herself at her feet, clasped her hands together, and lifted her sweet pale face and tearful eyes. For an instant the mother's face grew dark with passion; then she made a movement as if she were about to spurn the supplicant indignantly, when Charles sprang before her, and lifting Ellen in his arms, bore her from the house, and placed her half fainting in the carriage that still stood at the door. A hurried direction was given to the driver, who mounted his box and drove off to a hotel, where they passed the night, and, on the next morning, returned home to the city they had left on the previous day.

It was long before a smile lighted the countenance of the young bride. In silence she upbraided herself for having been the cause of estranging from each other mother and son.

"It was wrong," she said, in a sad tone, when, after the passage of a month, the subject was conversed about between them with more than usual calmness. "You should, first of all, have written to your mother, and asked her consent."

"But I knew she would not give it. I knew her peculiar prejudices too well. My only hope was the impression your dear face would make upon her. I was sure that for her to see you would be to love you. But I was mistaken."

"Alas! too sadly mistaken. We have made her unhappy through life. Oh! how that thought distresses me."

"She deserves all the unhappiness she may feel. For me, I do not pity her." Charles Linden said this with a good deal of bitterness.

"Oh! Charles—do not speak so—do not feel so. She is your mother, and you acted against what you knew to be one of her strongest prejudices," Ellen said earnestly. "I do not feel angry with her. When I think of her, it is with grief, that she is unhappy. The time may yet come— pray heaven it come quickly!—when she will feel differently toward one whose heart she does not know—when she will love me as a mother."

"She does not deserve the love of one like you," was the bitterly spoken reply.

"Ah, Charles! why will you speak so? It is not right."

"I can no more help it than I can help feeling and thinking, Ellen. I am indignant, and I must express my feelings. What a poor substitute is birth, or family connexion, or standing in society for a mother to offer to her son, in the place of a pure heart that can love fervently. If I had yielded to dictation on this subject, I would long ago have been the unhappy husband of a vain, selfish, proud creature, whom I never could have loved. No—no—Ellen. I cannot help being angry, if I may so speak, at the thought of such unjust, such unwise assumption of the prerogative in a parent. It is God who joins together in orderly marriage—not man; and when man attempts to assume the place of God in this matter, his work is evil. I would give my child, were I a parent, all the light, all the intelligence in my power to give him, and then let him choose for himself. To do more, would be, in my opinion, a sin against God, and, as such, I would shun it with horror."

In time, the deep affliction of mind which Ellen had experienced subsided. She felt the injustice of Mrs. Linden's conduct, and, though she had no indignant nor unkind feeling toward her, she thought of her without an emotion of filial regard. Year after year went by, and, as no notice whatever was taken of Charles and his wife by Mrs. Linden, they did not again venture near her, nor take any pains to conciliate her favour. Her treatment of Ellen had so outraged her son, that he tried to forget that he had a mother; for he could not think of her without a bitterness which he did not wish to feel. The only means of knowing what took place at home was through his sister, between whom and himself had always existed a warm affection. She wrote to him frequently, and he as well as his wife wrote to her often. Their letters to her were, at her request, sent under cover to a friend, to prevent the unpleasant consequences that would ensue, should the proud, overbearing mother become aware of the correspondence.

From his sister, who had something of his own independence of feeling, Charles learned, that his brother William, at his mother's instance, was about to marry Antoinette Billings. And, also, that an application had been made to the legislature to have his name changed to Beauchamp, his mother's family name. As an inducement for him to gratify her pride in this thing, Mrs. Linden had promised William, that, on the very day that the legislature granted the petition, she should transfer to him the whole amount of her property, with the exception of about twenty thousand dollars. Subsequently, Charles learned that the name of his brother had been changed; that the marriage had taken place; and that his mother had relinquished all her property, with a small reservation, into the hands of her son. All this took place within three years after his marriage.

The next intelligence was of an attempt being made to force Florence, his sister, into a marriage most repugnant to her feelings. This aroused his indignation afresh. He wrote to her strongly, and conjured her by every high and holy consideration not to permit the sacrifice to take place. Florence possessed too much of the same spirit that he did to yield tamely in a matter like this. His frequent letters strengthened her to resist all the attempts of her mother and brother to induce her to yield to their mercenary wishes. Finding that she was firm, a system of persecution, in the hope of forcing her to an assent, was commenced against her. As soon as Charles learned this, he went immediately to P—, and saw Florence at the home of a mutual friend. He had little difficulty in persuading her to return home with him. Neither her mother nor William showed her any real affection, and they were both plotting against her happiness for life. On the other hand, there had always been between her and Charles a deep attachment. She not only loved him, but confided in him. She had never seen his wife; but Charles had written so much about her, and Ellen's letters had pictured a mind so gentle, so good, that Florence loved her only less than she loved her brother. And there was another there to love, of whom she had heard much—a fair-haired girl named Florence. Is it a subject of wonder that she fled from her mother, to find a paradise in comparison to what she had left, in the home of Charles and his pure-hearted companion? We think not.

The meeting between her and Ellen was one in which both their hearts overflowed—in which affections mingled—in which two loving spirits became united in bonds that nothing could break.

We turn, now, to the disappointed Mrs. Linden. Knowing that to inform her mother of the step she had resolved to take would do no good, but only cause her to endure a storm of passion, Florence left home without the slightest intimation of her purpose.

Mrs. Linden, in settling upon her son William her whole estate, with the small reservation before mentioned, gave up to him the splendid mansion in which she lived, with its costly furniture—and the entire control of it, as a matter that followed of course, to his young wife. Many months had not passed, before doubts of the propriety of what she had done began to creep into the mind of Mrs. Linden. Her pride of family had been gratified—but already had her pride of independence been assailed. It was plain that she was not now of as much importance in the eyes of her son as before. As to Antoinette, the more she came intimately in contact with her, the less she liked her. She found little in her that she could love. The scheme of marrying Florence to a young man of "one of the first families" (the only recommendation he had) was heartily entered into by this worthy trio, and while there was a prospect of its accomplishment, they drew together with much appearance of harmony.

The end united them. But after Florence had broken away from the toils they had been throwing around her, and they became satisfied from the strong independent letters which she sent home, that all hope of bending her to their wishes was at an end, the true character of each began to show itself more fully.

Mrs. Linden had an imperious will. She had always exercised over her children a rigid control, at the same time that in their earlier years she had won their affections. The freedom of mature years, and the sense of individual responsibility which it brings, caused all of them to rebel against the continued exercise of parental domination. In the case of Charles and Florence, the effect was a broad separation. William had sinister ends to gain in yielding a passive obedience to his mother's will. When the bulk of her property was transferred to him, those ends were gained, and he felt no longer disposed to suffer any encroachment upon his freedom. In one act of obedience he had fulfilled all obligations of filial duty, and was not disposed to trouble himself further. He had consented to give up his father's name, and to marry a woman for whom he had no affection, to please his mother and get an estate. The estate set off against these balanced the account; and now, there being nothing more to gain, he had nothing more to yield. When, therefore, after the design of marrying Florence to a man of "good family" had failed, the first effort on the part of his mother to exercise control over him was met in a very decided way. His wife, likewise, showed a disposition to make her keep in her own place. She was mistress in the house now, and she let it be clearly seen. It was not long before the mother's eyes were fully open to the folly she had committed. But true sight had come too late. Reflection on the ungratefulness of her children aroused her indignation, instead of subduing her feelings. An open rupture ensued, and then came a separation. Mrs. Linden left the house of her son—but a short time before it was her own house—and took lodgings in the family of an old friend, with a heart full of bitterness toward her children. In Antoinette she had been miserably disappointed. A weak, vain, passionate, selfish creature, she had shown not the slightest regard for Mrs. Linden, but had exhibited toward her a most unamiable temper.

When it was communicated to Antoinette by her husband that his mother had left them, she tossed her head and said—"I'm glad to hear it."

"No, you must not say that," was William's reply, with an effort to look serious and offended.

"And why not? It's the truth. She has made herself as disagreeable as she could, ever since we were married, and I would be a hypocrite to say that I was not glad to be rid of her."

"She is my mother, and you must not speak so about her," returned William, now feeling really offended.

"How will you help it, pray?" was the stinging reply. And the ill-tempered creature looked at her husband with a curl of the lip.

Muttering a curse, he turned from her and left the house. The rage of a husband who is only restrained by the fear of disgrace from striking his wife, is impotent. His only resource is to fly from the object of indignation. So felt and acted William Beauchamp. A mere wordy contention with his wife, experience had already proved to him, would be an inglorious one.

Fearing, from his knowledge of his brother's character and disposition, a result, sooner or later, like that which had taken place,

Charles Linden, although he had no correspondence with any of his family, had the most accurate information from a friend of all that transpired at P——.

One evening, on coming home from business and joining his wife and sister, between whom love had grown into a strong uniting bond, he said—"I have rather painful news from P——."

"What is it?" was asked by both Ellen and Florence, with anxious concern on both their faces.

"Mother has separated herself from William and his wife."

"What I have been expecting to hear almost every day," Florence replied. "Antoinette has never treated mother as if she had the slightest regard for her. As to love, she has but one object upon which to lavish it— that is herself. She cares no more for William than she does for mother, and is only bound to him by external consideration. But where has mother gone?"

"To the house of Mrs. R——."

"An old friend?"

"Yes. But she must be very unhappy."

"Miserable." And tears came to the eyes of Ellen.

"In the end, it will no doubt be best for her, Florence," said the brother. "She will suffer acutely, but her false views of life, let us hope, will be corrected, and then we shall have it in our power to make her last days the best and happiest of her life."

"Oh, how gladly will I join in that work!" Mrs. Linden said, with a glow of pure enthusiasm on her face. "Write to her, dear husband, at once, and tell her that our home shall be her home, and that we will love her with an unwavering love."

"Not yet, dear," returned Charles Linden, in a voice scarcely audible from emotion, turning to Ellen and regarding her a moment with a look of loving approval. "Not yet; the time for that will come, but it is not now. My mother's heart is full of haughty pride, and she would spurn, indignantly, any overtures we might make."

Much conversation passed as to what should be their future conduct in regard to the mother. Ellen was anxious to make advances at once, but the husband and his sister, who knew Mrs. Linden much better than she did, objected.

"Time will indicate what is right for us to do," her husband said. "Let us keep our hearts willing, and we shall have the opportunity to act before many years pass by."

"Years?" said Ellen, in an earnest, doubting voice.

"It may be only months, dear, and yet it may be years. It takes time to break a haughty will, to humble a proud heart; but you shall yet see the day when my mother will love you for yourself alone."

"Heaven grant that it may come soon!" was the fervent response.

Many months passed away, and yet the mother and son remained as before—unreconciled. He had kept himself accurately informed in regard to her—that is, accurately informed as it was possible for him to be. During that time, she had never been seen abroad. Those who had met her, represented her as being greatly changed; all the softness of character that had been assumed in her intercourse with the world had been laid aside; she was silent, cold, and stern to all who met her.

Deeply did this intelligence afflict Charles, and he yearned to draw near to his mother; but he feared to do so, lest, in her haughty pride, she should throw him off again, and thus render a reconciliation still more difficult, if not impossible.

While in this state of doubt, affairs assumed a new feature. Charles received a letter from a friend, stating that the banking institution, in the stocks of which his mother's entire property was invested, had failed, and that she was penniless.

"O Charles, go to her at once!" was the exclamation of Ellen, the moment her husband read to her the intelligence. "It is time now; all else has failed her."

"I do not know," he said, doubtingly. "This circumstance will make William sensible of his duty; he will, no doubt, restore her a part of the property received from her hands. This is the least he can do."

Florence differed with her brother. She did not believe that either William or his wife would regard their mother in any way; both were too selfish and too unforgiving. Much was said all around, but no clear course of action was perceived.

"I'll tell you what you can do," spoke up Mrs. Linden, her eyes sparkling. A thought had flashed over her mind.

"What is it, Ellen?" asked her husband.

"You can send her, under a blank envelope, a thousand dollars or more, and thus keep her above the bitter feeling of dependence. More can be sent when more is required."

"True! true!" was the husband's quick reply. "And I will do it."

When the news of the failure of the bank in which the little remnant of her property was contained reached the ears of Mrs. Linden, her spirits sank. Pride had kept her up before; but now her haughty self-dependence, her indignation, her bitterness of feeling toward her children, gave way, and, in conscious weakness, she bowed her head and prayed for oblivion. She felt deserted by all; but indignation at this desertion was not the feeling that ruled in her heart; she felt weak, lonely, and powerless. From a high position, which she had held with imperious pride, she had fallen almost suddenly into obscurity, desertion, and dependence. A week passed, and she began to think of her children; none of them had yet come near her, or inquired for her. The thoughts of William and his heartless wife caused old feelings of indignation to awaken and burn; but when the image of Charles and Florence came up before her mind, her eyes were ready to overflow. It was now that she remembered, with changed emotions, the cruel manner in which she had spurned Charles and the wife of his bosom. A sigh struggled up from her heart, and she leaned down her face upon the table before which she was sitting. Just at this time, a small sealed package was handed to her. She broke it open carelessly; but its contents made her heart bound, coming as they did just at that crisis. Under cover was a bank-bill amounting to one thousand dollars, and this memorandum—"It is yours."

Quickly turning to the direction, she read it over two or three times before satisfying herself that there was no mistake. Then she examined the writing within and without closely, in order to ascertain, if possible, from whom the timely aid had come, but without arriving at any certain conclusion.

This incident caused a new train of thoughts to pass through the mind of Mrs. Linden. It brought before her, she could not tell why, the image of her son Charles with greater distinctness than ever; and with that came thoughts of his wife, and regret that she had thrown her off with such cruel anger. Acute pain of mind succeeded to this. She saw more clearly her own position in that act, and felt deeply the wrong she had committed.

"I will write to my son at once and ask his forgiveness, and that of his wife, whom I have wronged," she said, with a suddenly formed resolution. But pride rushed up instantly.

"No, no," it objected; "not now. You should have done this before: it is too late; they will not believe you sincere."

A painful conflict ensued, which continued with increasing violence until, in consequence of prolonged mental excitement, a slow nervous fever took hold of Mrs. Linden's physical system, and in a short time reduced her to a very critical state. Intelligence of this was conveyed to her son William, but, for some cause or other, neither himself nor wife visited her. At the end of a week she was so low as to be considered in great danger; she, no longer recognised the person of her attendant, or appeared to be conscious of what was passing around her.

A letter from a friend, through whom he was kept informed of all that occurred to her, apprized Charles Linden of his mother's critical situation.

"Florence," said he to his sister, in reading the letter to her and his wife, "I think you and I should go to P—immediately. You can be mother's nurse until she recovers, and then it may not be hard to reconcile all that is past."

Ellen looked earnestly in the face of her husband; something was on her tongue, but she appeared to hesitate about giving it utterance.

"Does not that meet your approval?" asked Charles.

"Why may not I be the nurse?" was asked in hesitating tones.

"You!" said Charles, in a voice of surprise. "That should be the duty of Florence."

"And my privilege," returned Ellen, speaking more firmly.

"What good would be the result?"

"Great good, I trust. Let me go and be the angel to her sick-chamber. She is too ill to notice any one; she will not, therefore, perceive that a stranger is ministering to her. As she begins to recover, and I have an inward assurance that she will, I will bestow upon her the most assiduous attentions. I will inspire her heart with grateful affection for one whom she knows not; and when she asks for my name, I will conceal it until the right moment, and then throw myself at her feet and call her mother. Oh! let it be my task to watch in her sick-chamber."

Neither Charles nor his sister said one word in opposition. On the next day, they all started for P—. Charles Linden went with his excellent wife to the house where his mother was residing with an old friend, and opened to this friend their wishes. She readily entered into their plans, and Ellen was at once constituted nurse.

For the first two days, there were but few encouraging symptoms. Mrs. Linden was in a very critical situation. At the end of a week, the fever abated, leaving the patient as helpless as an infant, and with scarcely more consciousness of external things. During this time, Ellen attended her with some of the feeling with which a mother watches over her babe. Gradually the life-current in the veins of the sick woman became fuller and stronger. Gradually her mind acquired the power of acting through the external senses. Ellen perceived this. Now had come the ardently hoped-for time. With a noiseless step, with a voice low and tender, with hands that did their office almost caressingly, she anticipated and met every want of the invalid.

As light began again to dawn upon the mind of Mrs. Linden, she could not but notice the sweet-faced, gentle, assiduous stranger who had become her nurse. Her first feeling was one of gratitude, blended with affection. Never before had any one been so devoted to her; never before had any one appeared to regard her with such a real wish to do her good.

"What is your name, my dear?" she asked one day, in a feeble voice, looking up into her face.

A warm flush came over the cheeks of Ellen; her eyes dropped to the floor. She hesitated for several moments; then she replied in a low voice—"Ellen."

Mrs. Linden looked at her earnestly, but said nothing in reply.

"Who is this nurse you have been so kind to procure for me?" Mrs. Linden said to her friend, a few days subsequently. She had gained much in a short time.

"She is a stranger to me. I never saw her before she came and said that she had heard that there was a sick lady here who wished a nurse."

"She did?"

"Yes."

"She must be an angel in disguise, then."

"So I should think," returned her friend. "I have never met a lovelier person. Her face is sweetness itself; her manners are full of ease and grace, and her heart seems a deep well of love to all."

"Who can she be? Where did she come from? I feel toward her as if she were my own child."

"But she is only a nurse," said her friend. "Do not forget that, nor your station in society."

Mrs. Linden shook her head and murmured—"I have never found one like her in the highest places; no, not even in my own children. Station in society! Ah! my friend, that delusion has passed."

As Mrs. Linden recovered more and more, Ellen remained with her, waiting only for a good opportunity to make herself known. She did not wish to do this until she was sure that she had awakened a feeling of affection in her mother's bosom.

Mrs. Linden had been sitting up for two or three days, so far had she recovered, and yet Ellen did not feel that it was safe to venture a full declaration of the truth.

Up to this time, neither William nor his wife had visited her, nor sent to inquire about her. This fact Mrs. Linden knew, for she had asked about it particularly. The name of Charles was never mentioned.

In order to try its effect, Ellen said to her—"You are better now, Mrs. Linden, and will be well in a little while. You do not need me any longer. I will leave you to-morrow."

"Leave me!" ejaculated Mrs. Linden. "Oh, no, Ellen, you must not leave me; I cannot do without you. You must stay with me always."

"You would soon tire of such a one as I am."

"Never, my good girl, never! You shall always remain with me. You shall be—not my nurse, but my child."

Mrs. Linden's voice trembled.

Ellen could hardly help throwing herself at her feet, and declaring that she was really her child; but she controlled herself, and replied—"That cannot be, madam; I have other duties to perform."

"You have? What? To whom?"

"To my husband and children."

"Gracious heaven! what do you mean? Who are you?"

"One who loved you before she ever saw you. One who loves you now."

"Speak, child! oh, speak!" exclaimed Mrs. Linden, turning suddenly pale, and grasping hold of Ellen with both her hands. "Who are you? What interest have you in me? Speak!"

"Do you love me?" asked Ellen, in a husky whisper.

"Love you! You have forced me to love you; but speak out. Who are you?"

"Your daughter," was faintly replied.

"Who?"

"The wife of one who has never ceased to love you; the wife of Charles Linden."

Mrs. Linden seemed paralyzed for some moments at this declaration. Her face became pale—her eye fell to the floor—she sat like one in a dream.

"Dear mother!" plead the anxious wife, sinking on her knees, "will you not forgive your son? Will you not forgive me that I loved him so well? If you knew how much we love you—how anxious we are to make you happy, you would instantly relent."

"My child! Oh, can it be true?" This was said in a choking voice by Mrs. Linden, as she threw her arms around Ellen and held her to her bosom. In a few moments she withdrew herself, and fixed her eyes long and earnestly upon Ellen's face.

"Ah! what a loving heart have I wronged!" she murmured, putting her hand upon the brow of her new-found child, tenderly. Then she drew her again almost convulsively to her bosom.

All that was passing within was heard without, for Charles and his sister were at the door: they entered at this moment.

"My mother!" exclaimed Charles, springing towards her.

"My son—my dear son! God bless you, and this dear child, who has watched for days and nights like an angel about my pillow."

The mother and son were in each other's arms in a moment. All was forgiven.

From that hour, the proud woman of the world saw with a purified vision. From that hour, she knew the worth of a pure heart.

SMITH AND JONES; OR, THE TOWN LOT.

ONCE upon a time, it happened that the men who governed in the municipal affairs of a certain growing town in the West, resolved, in grave deliberation assembled, to purchase a five-acre lot at the north end of the city—recently incorporated—and have it improved for a park or public square. Now, it also happened, that all the saleable ground lying north of the city was owned by a man named Smith—a shrewd, wide-awake individual, whose motto was,

"Every man for himself," with an occasional addition about a certain gentleman in black taking "the hindmost."

Smith, it may be mentioned, was secretly at the bottom of this scheme for a public square, and had himself suggested the matter to an influential member of the council; not that he was moved by what is denominated public spirit—no; the spring of action in the case was merely "private spirit," or a regard for his own good. If the council decided upon a public square, he was the man from whom the ground would have to be bought; and he was the man who could get his own price therefor.

As we have said, the park was decided upon, and a committee of two appointed, whose business it was to see Smith and arrange with him for the purchase of a suitable lot of ground. In due form the committee called upon the landholder, who was fully prepared for the interview.

"You are the owner of those lots at the north end?" said the spokesman of the committee.

"I am," replied Smith, with becoming gravity.

"Will you sell a portion of ground, say five acres, to the city?"

"For what purpose?" Smith knew very well for what purpose the land was wanted.

"We have decided to set apart about five acres of ground, and improve it as a kind of park, or public promenade."

"Have you, indeed? Well, I like that," said Smith, with animation. "It shows the right kind of public spirit."

"We have, moreover, decided that the best location will be at the north end of the town."

"Decidedly my own opinion," returned Smith.

"Will you sell us the required acres?" asked one of the councilmen.

"That will depend somewhat upon where you wish to locate the park."

The particular location was named.

"The very spot," replied Smith, promptly, "upon which I have decided to erect four rows of dwellings."

"But it is too far out for that," was naturally objected.

"Oh, no. Not a rod. The city is rapidly growing in that direction. I have only to put up the dwellings referred to, and dozens will be anxious to purchase lots, and build all around them. Won't the ground to the left of that you speak of answer as well?"

But the committee replied in the negative. The lot they had mentioned was the one decided upon as most suited for the purpose, and they were not prepared to think of any other location.

All this Smith understood very well. He was not only willing, but anxious for the city to purchase the lot they were negotiating for. All he wanted was to get a good round price for the same—say four or five times the real value. So he feigned indifference, and threw difficulties in the way.

A few years previous to this time, Smith had purchased a considerable tract of land at the north of the then flourishing village, at fifty dollars an acre. Its present value was about three hundred dollars an acre.

After a good deal of talk on both sides, Smith finally agreed to sell the particular lot pitched upon. The next thing was to arrange as to price.

"At what do you hold this ground per acre?"

It was some time before Smith answered this question. His eyes were cast upon the floor, and earnestly did he enter into debate with himself as to the value he should place upon the lot. At first, he thought of five hundred dollars per acre. But his cupidity soon tempted him to advance on that sum, although, a month before, he would have caught at such an offer. Then he advanced to six, to seven, and to eight hundred. And still he felt undecided.

"I can get my own price," said he to himself. "The city has to pay, and I might just as well get a large sum as a small one."

"For what price will you sell?" The question was repeated.

"I must have a good price."

"We are willing to pay what is fair and right."

"Of course. No doubt you have fixed a limit to which you will go."

"Not exactly that," said one of the gentlemen.

"Are you prepared to make an offer?"

"We are prepared to hear your price, and to make a report thereon," was replied.

"That's a very valuable lot of ground," said Smith.

"Name your price," returned one of the committee men, a little impatiently.

Thus brought up to the point, Smith, after thinking hurriedly for a few moments, said—

"One thousand dollars an acre."

Both the men shook their heads in a very positive way. Smith said that it was the lowest he would take; and so the conference ended.

At the next meeting of the city councils, a report on the town lot was made, and the extraordinary demand of Smith canvassed. It was unanimously decided not to make the proposed purchase.

When this decision reached the landholder, he was considerably disappointed. He wanted money badly, and would have "jumped at" two thousand dollars for the five-acre lot, if satisfied that it would bring no more. But, when the city came forward as a purchaser, his cupidity was subjected to a very strong temptation. He believed that he could get five thousand dollars as easily as two; and quieted his conscience by the salvo— "An article is always worth what it will bring."

A week or two went by, and Smith was about calling upon one of the members of the council, to say that, if the city really wanted the lot, he would sell at their price, leaving it with the council to act justly and generously, when a friend said to him—

"I hear that the council had the subject of a public square under consideration again this morning."

"Indeed!" Smith was visibly excited, though he tried to appear calm.

"Yes; and I also hear that they have decided to pay the extravagant price you asked for a lot of ground at the north end of the city."

"A thousand dollars an acre?"

"Yes."

"Its real value, and not a cent more," said Smith.

"People differ about that. However, you are lucky," the friend replied. "The city is able to pay."

"So I think. And I mean they shall pay."

Before the committee to whom the matter was given in charge had time to call upon Smith and close with him for the lot, that gentleman had concluded in his own mind that it would be just as easy to get twelve hundred dollars an acre as a thousand. It was plain that the council were bent upon having the ground, and would pay a round sum for it. It was just the spot for a public square; and the city must become the owner. So, when he was called upon by the gentlemen, and they said to him—

"We are authorized to pay you your price," he promptly answered—

"The offer is no longer open. You declined it when it was made. My price for that property is now twelve hundred dollars an acre."

The men offered remonstrance; but it was of no avail. Smith believed that he could get six thousand dollars for the ground as easily as five thousand. The city must have the lot, and would pay almost any price.

"I hardly think it right, Mr. Smith," said one of his visitors, "for you to take such an advantage. This square is for the public good."

"Let the public pay, then," was the unhesitating answer. "The public is able enough."

"The location of this park at the north end of the city will greatly improve the value of your other property."

This Smith understood very well. But he replied—

"I'm not so sure of that. I have some very strong doubts on the subject. It's my opinion that the buildings I contemplated erecting will be far more to my advantage. Be that as it may, however, I am decided in selling for nothing less than six thousand dollars."

"We are only authorized to pay five thousand," replied the committee. "If you agree to take that sum, we will close the bargain on the spot."

Five thousand dollars was a large sum of money, and Smith felt strongly tempted to close in with the liberal offer. But six thousand loomed up before his imagination still more temptingly.

"I can get it," said he to himself; "and the property is worth what it will bring."

So he positively refused to sell it at a thousand dollars per acre.

"At twelve hundred, you will sell?" remarked one of the committee, as they were about retiring.

"Yes. I will take twelve hundred the acre. That is the lowest rate; and I am not anxious, even at that price. I can do quite as well by keeping it in my own possession. But, as you seem so bent on having it, I will not stand in your way. When will the council meet again?"

"Not until next week."

"Very well. If they then accept my offer, all will be right. But, understand me; if they do not accept, the offer no longer remains open. It is a matter of no moment to me which way the thing goes."

It was a matter of moment to Smith, for all this assertion—a matter of very great moment. He had several thousand dollars to pay in the course of the next few months on land purchases, and no way to meet the payments, except by mortgages or sales of property; and it may naturally be concluded that he suffered considerable uneasiness during the time which passed until the next meeting of the council.

Of course, the grasping disposition shown by Smith became the town talk; and people said a good many hard things of him. Little, however, did he care, so that he secured six thousand dollars for a lot not worth more than two thousand.

Among other residents and property-holders in the town, was a simple-minded, true-hearted, honest man, named Jones. His father had left him a large farm, a goodly portion of which, in process of time, came to be included in the limits of the new city; and he found a much more profitable employment in selling building lots than in tilling the soil. The property of Mr. Jones lay at the west side of the town.

Now, when Mr. Jones heard of the exorbitant demand made by Smith for a five-acre lot, his honest heart throbbed with a feeling of indignation.

"I couldn't have believed it of him," said he. "Six thousand dollars! Preposterous! Why, I would give the city a lot of twice the size, and do it with pleasure."

"You would?" said a member of the council, who happened to hear this remark.

"Certainly, I would."

"You are really in earnest?"

"Undoubtedly. Go and select a public square from any of my unappropriated land on the west side of the city, and I will pass you the title, as a free gift, to-morrow, and feel pleasure in doing so."

"That is public spirit," said the councilman.

"Call it what you will. I am pleased in making the offer."

Now, let it not be supposed that Mr. Jones was shrewdly calculating the advantage which would result to him from having a park at the west side of the city. No such thought had yet entered his mind. He spoke from the impulse of a generous feeling.

Time passed on, and the session-day of the council came round—a day to which Smith had looked forward with no ordinary feelings of interest, that were touched, at times, by the coldness of doubt and the agitation of uncertainty. Several times he had more than half repented of his refusal to accept the liberal offer of five thousand dollars, and of having fixed so positively upon six thousand as the "lowest figure."

The morning of the day passed, and Smith began to grow uneasy. He did not venture to seek for information as to the doings of the council, for that would be to expose the anxiety he felt in the result of their deliberations. Slowly the afternoon wore away, and it so happened that Smith did not meet any one of the councilmen; nor did he even know whether the council was still in session or not. As to making allusion to the subject of his anxious interest to any one, that was carefully avoided; for he knew that his exorbitant demand was the town talk—and he wished to affect the most perfect indifference on the subject.

The day closed, and not a whisper about the town-lot had come to the ears of Mr. Smith. What could it mean? Had his offer to sell at six thousand been rejected? The very thought caused his heart to grow heavy in his bosom. Six, seven, eight o'clock came, and still it was all dark with Mr. Smith. He could bear the suspense no longer, and so determined to call upon his neighbour Wilson, who was a member of the council, and learn from him what had been done.

So he called on Mr. Wilson.

"Ah, friend Smith," said the latter, "how are you, this evening?"

"Well, I thank you," returned Smith, feeling a certain oppression of the chest. "How are you?"

"Oh, very well."

Here, then, was a pause. After which, Smith said—

"About that ground of mine? What did you do?"

"Nothing," replied Wilson, coldly.

"Nothing, did you say?" Smith's voice was a little husky.

"No. You declined our offer;—or, rather, the high price fixed by yourself upon the land."

"You refused to buy it at five thousand when it was offered," said Smith.

"I know we did, because your demand was exorbitant."

"Oh, no, not at all," returned Smith, quickly.

"In that we only differ," said Wilson. "However, the council has decided not to pay you the price you ask."

"Unanimously?"

"There was not a dissenting voice."

Smith began to feel more and more uncomfortable.

"I might take something less," he ventured to say, in a low, hesitating voice.

"It is too late now," was Mr. Wilson's prompt reply.

"Too late! How so?"

"We have procured a lot."

"Mr. Wilson!" Poor Smith started to his feet in chagrin and astonishment.

"Yes; we have taken one of Jones's lots, on the west side of the city. A beautiful ten-acre lot."

"You have!" Smith was actually pale.

"We have; and the title-deeds are now being made out."

It was some time before Smith had sufficiently recovered from the stunning effect of this unlooked-for intelligence, to make the inquiry—

"And pray how much did Jones ask for his ten-acre lot?"

"He presented it to the city as a gift," replied the councilman.

"A gift! What folly!"

"No, not folly—but true worldly wisdom; though I believe Jones did not think of advantage to himself when he generously made the offer. He is worth twenty thousand dollars more to-day than he was yesterday, in the simple advanced value of his land for building-lots. And I know of no man in this town whose good fortune affects me with more pleasure."

Smith stole back to his home with a mountain of disappointment on his heart. In his cupidity, he had entirely overreached himself, and he saw that the consequences were to react upon all his future prosperity. The public square at the west end of the town would draw improvements in that direction all the while increasing the wealth of Mr. Jones, while lots in the north end would remain at present prices, or, it might be, take a downward range.

And so it proved. In ten years, Jones was the richest man in the town, while half of Smith's property had been sold for taxes. The five-acre lot passed from his hands, under the hammer, in the foreclosure of a mortgage, for one thousand dollars!

Thus it is that inordinate selfishness and cupidity overreach themselves; while the liberal man deviseth liberal things, and is sustained thereby.

HE MUST HAVE MEANT ME.

"HOW do you like our new preacher?" was asked by one member of another, as they walked home from church.

"Only so so," was replied.

"He cuts close," remarked the first speaker.

"Yes, a little too close."

"I don't know about that. I like to see the truth brought home to the heart and conscience."

"So do I. But I object to personality."

"Personality!"

"Yes; I object to personality."

So does every one. Was Mr. C— personal?"

"I think so."

"That's hardly possible. He only arrived last week, and has not yet had time to become familiar with facts in the life of any one here. Moreover, a personal allusion in a first sermon, by a stranger, is something so out of place and indelicate, that I cannot for a moment believe that your inference is correct."

"While I have the best of reasons for believing that I complain of him justly. He's been long enough here to visit a certain family, fond of tittle-tattle, that I could name."

"The Harrisons?"

"Yes."

"I hope you are mistaken."

"No; I am not mistaken. C— was personal, and distinctly so. And the Harrisons are at the bottom of the matter. To say the least, he has acted in very bad taste. Charity should have prompted him to wait until he could have heard both sides of the story."

"I agree with you, fully, if your allegation be correct. But I must hope that you are in error."

"No. I have the best of reasons for what I allege."

"To whom did the personality apply?"

"To myself, if the truth must be spoken."

"Is it possible?"

"Yes—to myself."

"That places the matter in rather a serious light, Mr. Grant."

"It does. And I think I have reason to complain."

"You ought to be certain about this matter."

"I'm certain enough. When a man treads on your toe, you are likely to know it."

"It is barely possible that Mr. C— did not intend to designate you, or any one, in what he said."

"He *must* have meant me," replied Mr. Grant, with emphasis. "He couldn't have said what he did, unless he had been informed of certain things that have happened in this town. Had he not visited the Harrisons, I might have doubted. But that fact places the thing beyond a question."

"In what did the personality consist?"

"Did you not observe it?"

"No."

"Indeed!"

"I perceived no allusion to any one."

"There are plenty of others, no doubt, who did. I don't care to speak of it just now. But you'll hear about it. I noticed three or four turn and look at me while he was speaking. It will be a pleasant piece of gossip; but if Mr. C— doesn't take care, I'll make this place too hot to hold him. I'm not the one to be set up as a target for any whipper-snapper to fire at."

"Don't get excited, friend Grant. Wait awhile. I still think there is some mistake."

"I beg your pardon; there is no mistake about it. He meant me. Don't I know? Can't I tell when a man points his finger at me in a public assembly?"

In his opinion, Mr. Grant was still further confirmed, ere he reached his home, by the peculiar way in which sundry members of the congregation looked at him. Of course, he was considerably disturbed on the subject; and felt a reasonable share of indignation. In the evening, he declined attending worship as an indication of his feelings on the subject; and he doubted not that the new preacher would note his absence and understand the cause.

About a year prior to this time, Mr. Grant, who was a manufacturing jeweller, was called upon by a gentleman, who desired him to make a solid gold wedding-ring. It was to be of the finest quality that could be worked, and to be unusually heavy. When the price was mentioned, the gentleman objected to it as high.

"Your neighbour, over the way," said the gentleman, "will make it for a dollar less than you ask."

"Not of solid gold," replied Mr. Grant.

"Oh, yes. I would have no other."

Mr. Grant knew that the ring could not be made of fine, solid gold, for the price his neighbour had agreed to take. And he knew, also, that in manufacturing it, his neighbour, if he took the order, would fill up the centre of the ring with solder—a common practice. On the spur of the moment, he determined to do the same thing, and therefore replied—

"Well, I suppose I must work as low as he does."

"The ring must be of solid gold, remember. I will have no other."

"That's understood, of course," replied the jeweller; adding to himself, "as solid as any one makes them."

The ring was manufactured at a reasonable profit, and the man got the full worth of his money; but not of solid gold. Silver solder composed the centre. But as the baser metal could not be detected by simple inspection or weighing, Mr. Grant felt secure in the cheat he had practised; and, quieted his conscience by assuming that he had given a full equivalent for the money received.

"He's just as well off as he would have been if he had gone to my neighbour over the way, as he called him," said he to himself, in the effort to quiet certain unpleasant sensations. "To suppose that he was going to get a solid ring at such a price! Does he think we jewellers steal our gold? Men will be humbugged, and there is no help for it."

Yet, for all this, Mr. Grant could not cast out the unpleasant feeling. He had done a thing so clearly wrong, that no attempt at self-justification gave his mind its former calmness.

"The ring is solid gold?" said the man, when he came for it.

"That was the contract," replied Mr. Grant, with a half-offended air, at the intimation conveyed in the tone of voice, that all might not be as agreed upon.

"Excuse me," remarked the man, apologetically; "but I am very particular about this matter, and would throw the ring into the street rather than use it, if not of solid gold."

"Gold rings are not given away," muttered Grant to himself, as the man left the shop.

Some days after this transaction, a man named Harrison, who belonged to the church of which Grant was a member, met him, when this little conversation took place.

"I sent you a customer last week," said Mr. Harrison.

"Ah! I'm very much obliged to you."

"A gentleman who wanted a gold ring. He asked me to give him the name of a jeweller upon whom he could depend. The ring, he said, must be solid, for a particular reason; and, as he was a stranger, he did not know who was to be trusted. I told him I would guaranty you for an honest man. That if you undertook to manufacture any article for him, he might rely upon its being done according to agreement."

While Harrison was uttering this undeserved compliment, it was with the utmost difficulty that Mr. Grant could keep the tell-tale blood from rushing to his face.

"He showed me the ring," continued Mr. Harrison. "It is a very handsome one."

"Was he satisfied with it?" asked Mr. Grant.

"Not fully."

"Why so?"

"He was afraid it might not be solid. In fact, so anxious was he on this point, that he took the ring to your neighbour, over the way, to get his opinion about it."

As Mr. Harrison said this, Grant was conscious that a betrayal of the truth was on his countenance.

"And, of course, Martin said the ring was not solid."

"No, he did not exactly say that. I went with the gentleman, at his request. Martin weighed the ring, and, after doing so, simply stated that gold of the quality of which the ring was made was worth a certain price per pennyweight. By multiplying the number of pennyweights contained in the ring with the price mentioned, he showed that you either lost one dollar on the ring, or filled the centre with some baser metal."

"Well?" The blood had, by this time, risen to the very brow of the jeweller.

"'Cut the ring,' said my friend. It was done, and, to my mortification and astonishment, it proved to be even as he had said. The ring was not solid!"

For some moments, Mr. Grant hung his head in painful confusion. Then, looking up, he said—

"It was his own fault."

"How so?" was inquired.

"He would not pay the price for a solid ring, and I could not give him my work for nothing."

"Did you ask him a fair price?"

"Yes; and he answered, that my neighbour over the way had offered to make him a solid ring, for just one dollar less. I knew exactly what kind of a ring Martin could and would furnish for that money, and made him one just like it. I gave him his money's worth, and a little over. He was not cheated."

"But he was deceived. How you could have done such a thing, brother Grant, is more than I can understand."

"I had to do it in self-defence; and this very Martin, who has been so ready to expose the little deception, made the act necessary."

"I'm sorry you should have done so. It was wrong," said Mr. Harrison.

"I'm ready to acknowledge that. But it's too late, now, to repair the error. I wish I'd had nothing to do with the matter."

"So do I," remarked Harrison.

This fretted the mind of Grant, and he replied, rather impatiently—

"Hereafter, I hope you'll send all customers of this kind to Martin. Dear knows, I don't want them!"

"I shall certainly be careful in this matter," coldly replied Harrison, and bowing formally, as he spoke, turned away, and left Grant in no very pleasant frame of mind. From that time there was a coldness between the two church members.

When Grant went to church on the next Sabbath, he noticed, as he approached the meeting-house door, Harrison standing in close conversation with one or two prominent members. As he approached, they looked toward him in a certain way that he did not like, and then, separating, entered the house before he came up. It was too evident that Harrison had been communicating the incident of the ring. But Grant was not surprised; he had expected nothing less. Still, he felt that his brother member had not done towards him in the matter as he would have liked himself done by. On entering the church, half a dozen persons turned and looked at him earnestly; while two or three whispered together, glancing towards him every now and then, and thus showing that he was the subject of conversation. As to the theme of discourse between them, his mind was in no doubt. The gold ring! Yes, that was it.

But little edified by the sermon was Mr. Grant on that morning; and, when the services were ended, he went quickly from the church, and took his way homeward without stopping, as on former occasions, to shake hands and pass a few words with friends and brethren.

It had been the custom of several leading members of the church to drop in occasionally, during the week, and chat with Grant for ten minutes or half an hour. But the time from Sunday to Sunday was passed without a single call from any one of them. The reason for this was no mystery to the jeweller's mind.

"I don't see that I've been guilty of such a terrible crime," said he to himself, feeling a little indignant on the subject. "The man got his money's worth; and, moreover, was served perfectly right. Did he suppose that he was going to get fine gold for the price of solder? If so, he found himself mistaken. As for Harrison, he's made himself remarkably busy about the matter. I would not trust him in a similar case. But it is so pleasant to discourse on evil in our neighbour. So very pleasant! The good he does is left to find its own way to the light as best it can; but let him commit a mistake or make a single false step, and it is preached from house-top."

When Grant and Harrison met, there was a mutual reserve and coldness.

"He is conscious, I am aware, of his wrong dealing," said the latter to himself, "and therefore shuns me."

"He is aware that he has tried to injure me," said the former, "and cannot, therefore, meet me as of old."

Two or three weeks passed before the friends who used to drop in to see him almost every day showed themselves in his shop, and then there was a too evident change of manner. They appeared distant and reserved, and he met them with a like exterior. His pride was touched.

"Just as they like," he said to himself. "I can get on without them. I presume, if all our hearts were laid open, mine would be found quite as good as theirs. As for Perkins and Marvel, they needn't set themselves up over me. I think I know them. Men who cut as close as they do in dealing, generally cut a little from the side that doesn't belong to them."

Perkins and Marvel, here alluded to, had long been on friendly terms with Mr. Grant—visiting at his shop—for the purpose of a little friendly chit-chat—every few days. But a coldness now took place, and, in a few weeks, they ceased their friendly calls.

In various other ways was Mr. Grant conscious of a reaction upon himself of his improper conduct. Hundreds of times did he mentally regret the weakness and love of gain which had prompted him to so far lose sight of what was just and honourable as to deceive a customer. So painful was his sense of mortification, that, for a time, he omitted to attend church on Sunday. Not only was he satisfied that every one in the congregation knew about the ring, but he could clearly perceive a change in the manner of his most intimate acquaintances who were members of the church.

Grant was not a man entirely sold to selfishness. He was not a deliberate wrong-doer, hiding his evil purposes and acts under a hypocritical exterior. He had conscience, and, at times, its voice was loud and distinct. He was, therefore, troubled about the ring as a fact indicating the state of his affections; as well as troubled about the condemnatory judgment of his brethren. There were fluctuations of state, of course, as there are with all of us. Sometimes he was in a state of humiliation on account of the evil he had done, and sometimes in a state of indignation at Harrison for having, been so eager to publish his fault from the house-top.

Gradually, however, the ever-recurring new purposes and interests which come to all in passing through life, threw the past with its influences into the shade, and the returns of states of mortification on account of the ring were less and less frequent. Mr. Grant resumed his attendance at church, and mingled, as of old, with his brethren; though in a rather more subdued and less confident spirit. That affair of the ring could not be entirely forgotten.

In due course of time, the minister on the station had to leave, and a new one was appointed by the conference to take his place. The Rev. Mr. C— arrived early in the week, and during the period that elapsed between that and the Sabbath, visited a good deal among the brethren. During that time, an evening was spent at Mr. Harrison's, but no one brought him around to introduce him to Mr. Grant. The jeweller felt this, and in his mind, in searching about for reasons, rested, very naturally, upon the affair of the gold ring, and he did not doubt but the occurrence had been fully related to Mr. C—.

Under this feeling, Mr. Grant went to church. His first sight of the new preacher was when he arose in the pulpit to give out the hymn. His countenance did not make a very favourable impression, but his voice, when he commenced reading the hymn, had a tone and a modulation that were pleasing. The subject of the discourse which followed was practical, and had reference to a man's conduct towards his fellow-man in the common affairs of life. From general propositions, the minister, after entering upon his sermon, came down to things particular. He dwelt upon the love of dominion so deeply rooted in the human heart, and showed, in various ways, how it was exercised by individuals in all the grades of common society.

"A more deeply-rooted evil than this," he went on to say, "is theft. We all inherit, in a greater or less degree, the desire to possess our neighbour's goods; and, with the earliest development of the mind, comes the activity of that desire. It is seen in the child when he appropriates the plaything of another child, and in the so-called good and honest citizen when, in bargaining, he secures an advantage at the expense of his brother."

Descending, gradually, to the introduction of particular forms of overreaching as practised in trade, all of which Mr. C— designated as instances of theft, he finally brought forward an instance so nearly resembling the one in which Mr. Grant had been engaged, that the latter felt himself, as has been seen, particularly pointed out, and left the church at the close of the service in a state of excitement and indignation. To have that old matter, about which he had already suffered enough, "raked over," as he said, "and exposed to light again," was a little more than he was disposed to submit to with patience. As has been seen, he did not conceal what was in his mind.

On Monday, a brother-member of the church dropped in to see the jeweller.

"How did you like Mr. C—?" was the natural inquiry.

"Not at all," replied Mr. Grant, in a positive tone.

"You didn't? Why, I was delighted with him! What is your objection?"

"He was personal in his discourse."

"I perceived nothing personal."

"Though I did, and of the grossest kind."

"How was it possible for a stranger like Mr. C— to be personal? He knows nothing of the characters or conduct of individuals here."

"Strangers generally have quick ears, and there are always plenty of news-venders to fill them. He's been with the Harrisons, and we all know what they are."

"To whom did he refer?" was asked.

"He referred to me."

"To you?"

"Certainly he did. And I don't like it at all. That's not the way to preach the gospel. This running off with one side of a story, and, taking all for granted, holding a man up to public odium, is not, as I conceive, following in the footsteps of our Great Master."

"I'm sorry you should have taken up such an impression," was replied to this. "I cannot believe that Mr. C— really intended to hold you up to public odium. He couldn't have meant to designate you."

"He must have meant me. Don't I know?"

So another and another objection was made to Mr. C— on the same ground; and before the week was out, it was pretty widely known that the new preacher had indulged in reprehensible personalities. Some said this was an error in the preacher; others, that he was highly blamable; while others affirmed that there must be some mistake about the matter.

On the following Sunday, Mr. Grant was absent from his usual place in the church. It would do him no good to sit under the ministry of Mr. C—.

During the week that followed, two of the official members called upon the jeweller to make inquiries about the alleged personalities. Grant was, by this time, pretty sore on the subject, and when allusion was made to it, he gave his opinion of the preacher in no very choice language.

"In what did this personality consist?" asked one of the visitors.

"It's hardly necessary to ask that question," replied Grant.

"It is for me. No one, whom I have yet seen, has been able to give me any information on the subject."

"If you ask Mr. C—, he will enlighten you."

"I have already done so."

"You have?"

"Yes."

"What was his reply?"

"That he is innocent of the personality laid to his charge."

"Did you mention my name?"

"I did."

"Well?"

"He had not even heard of you as a member of the church here."

"I can hardly credit that, after what he said."

"You will, at least, give him the chance of vindication. He is now at my house, and has expressed a wish to see you."

"I don't know that any good will grow out of seeing him," said Mr. Grant, who felt but little inclined to meet the preacher.

"I'm sorry to hear you say that, Mr. Grant. You have made a complaint against Mr. C—, and when he wishes to confer with you on the subject, you decline, under the assumption that no good can arise from it. This is not right; and I hope you will think better of it."

"Perhaps it isn't right; but so it is. At present, I do not wish to see him. I may feel differently to-morrow."

"Shall we call upon-you in the morning?"

"If you please to do so."

"Very well."

And the two official members departed.

No sooner were they gone, than Mr. Grant put or his hat and left his shop. He went direct to the store of Mr. Harrison.

"You are just the man I was thinking about," said the latter, as the jeweller entered. "What is all this trouble about you and Mr. C—? I hear some rumour of it at every turn."

"That is just what I have come to see you about."

"Very well; what can I do in the matter? Mr. C—, you allege, has held you up in the congregation to public odium?"

"I do."

"In what way?"

"Strange that you should ask the question."

"Why so? What have I to do with it?"

"A great deal," said Grant, his brows falling as he spoke.

"I must plead innocence until shown my guilt. So far, I have not even been able to learn in what the allusion to yourself consisted."

"*You* have not?"

"No."

Grant stood, tightly compressing his lips, for some moments. He then said:

"You remember that affair of the gold ring?"

"Very well."

"You mentioned this to C—."

"No. Nor to a living soul since the occurrence of the fact."

"What?"

"Nothing on that subject has ever passed my lips. I believed that you saw and repented of your error, and in honour and in conscience refrained from even the remotest allusion to the subject."

"How, then, did Mr. C— become cognisant of the fact?"

"If cognisant all, it was from another source than the one you supposed."

"I never mentioned it. You were the only one to whom the circumstance was communicated. How, then, could the matter have gotten abroad?"

"I don't believe a single member of the congregation ever heard of it."

"Oh, yes, they have. These has been a marked change in the manner of very many towards me. So apparent was this at one time, that I absented myself from church, rather than encounter it."

"All your imagination, brother Grant, and nothing else. I believe that I mingle as freely with the congregation as any one, and I know that I never heard a breath against you. At present, every one is at a loss to know in what way Mr. C— pointed you out; he is equally in the dark."

"I was sure he meant me. It was so plain," said Mr. Grant, his countenance falling, and his manner becoming subdued.

"There was nothing of the kind, you may depend upon it," replied Mr. Harrison.

"And you never spoke of it?"

"Never!"

"A guilty conscience, it is said, needs no accuser. The likeness to me was so strong, that I really thought the picture was sketched from myself as the original. Ah, me!"

"Had you not better call on Mr. C——?" asked Harrison.

"No, no. See him for me, if you please, and tell him that I am convinced of my error in supposing he pointed me out in the congregation. As to the particular allusion that I felt to be offensive, I hope you will still keep your own counsel. I did wrong, under temptation, and have suffered and repented in consequence. It can do no good to bring the matter to light now."

"None at all. I will not speak of it."

Nor did he. Many and various were the suggestions and suppositions of the congregation touching the nature of the preacher's personal allusion to the jeweller, and some dozen of little gossiping stories got into circulation; but the truth did not find its way to the light. And not until the day on which he was leaving the station for a new field of labour, did the preacher himself understand the matter; and then he had it from Mr. Grant's own lips.

FOR THE FUN OF IT.

"JUST look at them young lovers," said Harry Mears, glancing from his companion to a young man and maiden, who, for the moment unconscious that they were in the midst of a large company, were leaning towards each other, and looking into each other's faces in rather a remarkable manner. "Isn't it ridiculous? I thought Fisher had more sense than to do so. As to Clara Grant, she always was a little weak."

The friend looked at the couple an smiled. "It is ridiculous, certainly," he remarked. "Why havn't they sense enough to keep these little love-passages for private occasions?"

"Clara, with all her silliness used to be a right pleasant companion," said Mears. "But since this love affair between her and Fisher, she has become intolerably dull and uninteresting. She doesn't care a fig for anybody but him, and really appears to think it a task to be even polite to an old acquaintance. I don't think she has cause to be quite so elated with her conquest as this comes to; nor to feel that, in possessing the love of a man like Fisher, she is independent of the world, and may show off the indifference she feels to every one. Fisher is clever enough, but he is neither a Socrates nor a saint."

"He will suit her very well, I imagine."

"Yes; they will make a passable Darby and Joan, no doubt. Still, it always vexes me to see people, who pretend to any sense, acting in this way."

"I think it is more her fault than his."

"So do I. She has shown a disposition to bill and coo from the first. At Mangum's party, last week, she made me sick. I tried to get her hand for a dance, but no. Close to the side of Fisher she adhered, like a fixture, and could hardly force her lips into a smile for any one else. The gipsy! I'd punish her for all this, if I could just hit upon a good plan for doing it."

"Let me see," remarked the friend, dropping his head into a thoughtful position, "can't we devise a scheme for worrying her a little? She is certainly a fair subject. It would be fine sport."

"Yes, it would."

"She evidently thinks Fisher perfection."

"Oh, yes! There never was such a man before! She actually said to Caroline Lee, who was trying to jest with her a little, that Fisher was one of the most pure-minded, honourable young men living."

"Oh, dear."

"It is a fact."

"Was she serious?"

"Yes, indeed! Serious as the grave. Caroline was laughing to me about it. Nearly every one notices the silliness of her conduct, and the weakness she displays in forever talking about and praising him."

"I would like to run him down a little when she could overhear me, just for the fun of the thing."

"So would I. Capital! That will do, exactly. We must watch an opportunity, and if we can get within earshot of her, any time that she is by herself, we must abuse Fisher right and left, without appearing to notice that she is listening to what we say, or, indeed, anywhere near us."

"Right! That's the very thing. It will be capital fun."

Thus, the thoughtless young men, meddling themselves in a matter that did not concern them, determined upon a very questionable piece of folly. All that they said of the lovers was exaggeration. It was true that they did show rather more preference for each other in company than just accorded with good taste; but this, while it provoked a smile from the many, irritated only the few.

Clara Grant, notwithstanding the light manner in which the two young men had spoken of her, was a girl of good sense, good principles, and deep feeling, She had been several times addressed by young men before Fisher offered his hand; but, with all their attractions, there were defects about them, which her habits of close observation enabled her to see, that caused her to repel their advances, and in two instances to decline apparently very advantageous offers of marriage. In the integrity of Fisher's character, she had the most unbounded confidence; and she really believed, as she had said to Caroline Lee and others, that he was one of the purest-minded, most honourable young men living.

Judge, then, with what feelings she overheard, about half an hour after the plan to disturb her peace had been formed, the following conversation between Mears and his companion, carried on in low tones and in a confidential manner. She was sitting close to one side of the folding-doors that communicated between the parlours, and they were in the adjoining room, concealed from her by the half-partition, yet so close that every word they uttered was distinctly heard. Her attention was first arrested by hearing one of them say—

"If she knew Fisher as well as I do."

To which the other responded—

"Yes; or as well as I do. But, poor girl! it isn't expected that she is to know every thing about young men who visit her. It is better that she should not."

"Still, I am rather surprised that common report should not have given her more information about Fisher than she seems to possess."

"So am I. But she'll know him better one of these days."

"I'll warrant you that! Perhaps to her sorrow; though I hope things will turn out differently from what they now promise. Don't you think he is pretty well done with his wild oats?"

"Possibly. But time will tell."

"Yes, time proves all things."

Some one joining the young men at this point of their conversation, the subject was changed. Greatly amused at what they had done, they little thought how sad the effects of their unguarded words would be.

Five minutes afterwards, the young man named Mears, curious to see how Clara had been affected by what he knew she must have heard, moved to another part of the room, in order to observe her without attracting her attention. But she had left the place where she was sitting. His eye ranged around the room, but she was nowhere to be seen.

"I'm afraid we've hurt Clara more than we intended," he said, rejoining his friend. "She has vanished."

"Ah! Where's Fisher?"

"He's at the other end of the room."

"We didn't say any thing against the young man."

"Not in particular. We made no specifications. There was nothing that she could take hold of."

"No, of course not. But I wonder what is going to be the upshot of the matter?"

"Nothing very serious, I apprehend."

"No. I suppose she will go home and cry her eyes half out, and then conclude that, whatever Fisher may have been, he's perfection now. It's a first-rate joke, isn't it?"

Clara Grant had not only left the parlours, but soon after quietly left the house, and alone returned to her home. When her lover, shortly afterwards, searched through the rooms for her, she was nowhere to be seen.

"Where is Clara?" he asked of one and another. The answer was—

"I saw her here a moment since."

But it was soon very apparent that she was nowhere in the rooms now. Fisher moved about uneasy for half an hour. Still, not seeing her, he became anxious lest a sudden illness had caused her to retire from the company. More particular inquiries were made of the lady who had given the entertainment. She immediately ascertained for him that Clara was not in the house. One of the servants reported that a lady had gone away alone half an hour before. Fisher did not remain a single moment after receiving this intelligence, but went direct to the house of Clara's aunt, with whom she lived, and there ascertained that she had come home and retired to her room without seeing any of the family.

His inquiry whether she were ill, the servant could not answer.

"Have you seen anything of Clara yet?" asked the friend of Mears, with a smile, as they met about an hour after they had disturbed the peace of a trusting, innocent-minded girl, "just for the fun of it."

"I have not," replied Mears.

"Where's Fisher?"

"He is gone also."

"Ah, indeed! I'm sorry the matter was taken so seriously by the young lady. It was only a joke."

"Yes. That was all; and she ought to have known it."

On the next day, Fisher, who had spent a restless night, called to ask for Clara as early as he could do so with propriety.

"She wishes you to excuse her," said the servant, who had taken up his name to the young lady.

"Is she not well?" asked Fisher.

"She has not been out of her room this morning. I don't think she is very well."

The young man retired with a troubled feeling at his heart. In the evening he called again; but Clara sent him word, as she had done in the morning, that she wished to be excused.

In the mean time, the young lady was a prey to the most distressing doubts. What she had heard, vague as it was, fell like ice upon her heart. She had no reason to question what had been said, for it was, as far as appeared to her, the mere expression of a fact made in confidence by friend to friend without there being an object in view. If any one had come to her and talked to her after that manner, she would have rejected the allegations indignantly, and confidently pronounced them false. But they had met her in a shape so unexpected, and with so much seeming truth, that she was left no alternative but to believe.

Fisher called a third time; but still Clara declined seeing him. On the day after this last attempt, he received a note from her in these, to him, strange words:—

> "DEAR SIR:—Since I last met you, I have become satisfied that a marriage between us cannot prove a happy one. This conclusion is far more painful to me than it can possibly be to you. You, I trust, will soon be able to feel coldly towards her whose fickleness, as you will call it, so soon led her to change her mind; but a life-shadow is upon my heart. If you can forget me, do so, in justice to yourself. As for me, I feel that—but why should say this? Charles, do not seek to change the resolution I have taken, for you cannot; do not ask for explanations, for I can give none. May you be happier than I can ever be! Farewell.
>
> "CLARA."

"Madness!" exclaimed Charles Fisher, as he crumpled this letter in his hand. "Is there no faith in woman?"

He sought no explanation; he made no effort to change her resolution; he merely returned this brief answer—

"Clara, you are free."

It was quickly known among the circle of their friends that the engagement between Fisher and Clara had been broken off. Mears and his friend, it may be supposed, did not feel very comfortable when they heard this.

"I didn't think the silly girl would take it so seriously," remarked one to the other.

"No; it was a mere joke."

"But has turned out a very serious one."

"I guess they'll make it up again before long."

"I hope so. Who would have believed it was in her to take the matter so much at heart, or to act with so much decision and firmness? I really think better of the girl than I did before, although I pity her from my heart."

"Hadn't we better make an effort to undo the wrong we have done?"

"And expose ourselves? Oh, no! We must be as still as death on the subject. It is too serious an affair. We might get ourselves into trouble."

"True. But I cannot bear to think that others are suffering from an act of mine."

"It is not a pleasant consciousness, certainly. But still, to confess what we have done would place us in a very awkward position. In fact, not for the world would I have an exposure of this little act of folly take place. It would affect me in a certain quarter—where, I need not mention to you— in a way that might be exceedingly disagreeable."

"I didn't think of that. Yes, I agree with you that we had best keep quiet about it. I'm sorry; but it can't be helped now."

And so the matter was dismissed.

No one saw Clara Grant in company for the space of twelve months. When she did appear, all her old friends were struck with the great change in her appearance. As for Fisher, he had left the city some months before, and gone off to a Southern town, where, it was said, he was in good business.

The cause of estrangement between the lovers remained a mystery to every one. To all questions on the subject, Clara was silent. But that she was a sufferer every one could see.

"I wish that girl would fall in love with somebody and get married," Mears remarked to his friend, about two years after they had passed off upon Clara their good joke. "Her pale, quiet, suffering face haunts me wherever I go."

"So do I. Who could have believed that a mere joke would turn out so seriously?"

"I wonder if he is married yet?"

"It's doubtful. He appeared to take the matter quite as hard as she does."

"Well, it's a lesson to me."

"And to me, also."

And, with this not very satisfactory conclusion, the two friends dropped the subject. Both, since destroying, by a few words spoken in jest, the happiness of a loving couple, had wooed and won the maidens of their choice, and were now married. Both, up to this time, had carefully concealed from their wives the act of which they had been guilty.

After returning home from a pleasant company, one evening, at which Clara was present, the wife of Mears said to him—

"You did not seem to enjoy yourself to-night. Are you not well?"

"Oh, yes; I feel quite well," returned Mears.

"Why, then, did you look so sober?"

"I was not aware that I looked more so than usual."

"You did, then. And you look sober now. There must be some cause for this. What is it, dear?"

Mears was by no means ignorant of the fact that he felt sober. The presence of Clara distressed him more, instead of less, the oftener he met her. The question of his wife made him feel half inclined to tell her the truth. After thinking for a moment, he said—

"I have felt rather graver than usual to-night. Something brought to my recollection, too vividly, a little act of folly that has been attended with serious consequences."

His wife looked slightly alarmed.

"It was only a joke—just done for the fun of the thing; but it was taken, much to my surprise, seriously. I was innocent of any desire to wound; but a few light words have made two hearts wretched."

Mrs. Mears looked at her husband with surprise. He continued—

"You remember the strange misunderstanding that took place between Clara Grant and young Fisher, about two years ago?"

"Very well. Poor Clara has never been like herself since that time."

"I was the cause of it."

"You!" said the wife, in astonishment.

"Yes. Clara used to make herself quite conspicuous by the way she acted towards Fisher, with whom she was under an engagement of marriage. She hardly saw anybody in company but him. And, besides, she made bold to declare that he was about as near to perfection as it was possible for a young man to come. She was always talking about him to her young female friends, and praising him to the skies. Her silly speeches were every now and then reported, much to the amusement of young men to whose ears they happened to find their way. One evening, at a large party, she was, as usual, anchored by the side of her lover, and showing off her fondness for him in rather a ridiculous manner. A young friend and myself, who were rather amused at this, determined, in a thoughtless moment, that we would, just for the fun of the thing, run Fisher down in a confidential undertone to each other, yet loud enough for her to hear us, if a good opportunity for doing so offered. Before long, we noticed her sitting alone in a corner near one of the folding-doors. We managed to get near, yet so as not to appear to notice her, and then indulged in some light remarks about her lover, mainly to the effect that if his sweetheart knew him as well as we did, she might not think him quite so near perfection as she appeared to do. Shortly afterwards, I searched through the rooms for her in vain. From that night, the lovers never again met. Clara refused to see Fisher when he called on her the next day, and shortly afterwards requested him, in writing, to release her from her marriage-contract, without giving any reason for her change of mind."

"Henry," exclaimed Mrs. Mears, her voice and countenance expressing the painful surprise she felt, "why did you not immediately repair the wrong you had done?"

"How could I, without exposing myself, and causing perhaps a serious collision between me and Fisher?"

"You should have braved every consequence," replied Mrs. Mears, firmly, "rather than permitted two loving hearts to remain severed, when a word from you would have reunited them. How could you have hesitated a moment as to what was right to do? But it may not be too late yet. Clara must know the truth."

"Think what may be the consequence," said Nears.

"Think, rather, what *have been* the consequences," was the wife's reply.

It was in vain that Mears argued with his wife about the policy of letting the matter rest where it was. She was a woman, and could only feel how deeply Clara had been wronged, as well as the necessity for an immediate reparation of that wrong. For more than an hour, she argued the matter with her husband who finally consented that she should see Clara, and correct the serious error under which she had been labouring. Early on the next day, Mrs. Mears called upon the unhappy girl. A closer observation of her face than she had before made revealed deep marks of suffering.

"And all this 'for the fun of it!'" she could not help saying to herself with a feeling of sorrow. After conversing a short time with Clara, Mrs. Mears said—

"I heard something, last night, so nearly affecting your peace, that I have lost no time in seeing you."

"What is that?" asked Clara, a flush passing over her face.

"Two years ago, you were engaged in marriage to Mr. Fisher?"

Clara made no reply, but the flush faded from her face and her lips quivered slightly for a moment.

"From hearing two persons who were conversing about him make disparaging remarks, you were led to break off that engagement."

The face of Clara grew still paler, but she continued silent.

"By one of them, I am authorized to tell you that all they said was in mere jest. They knew you could hear what they said, and made the remarks purposely for your ear, in order to have a little sport. They never dreamed of your taking it so seriously."

A deep groan heaved the bosom of Clara; her head fell back, and her body drooped nervelessly. Mrs. Mears extended her hands quickly and saved her from falling to the floor.

"This, too, 'for the fun of it!'" she said to herself, bitterly, as she lifted the inanimate body of the poor girl in her arms, and laid it upon the sofa.

Without summoning any of the family, Mrs. Mears made use of every effort in her power to restore the circle of life. In this she was at last successful. When the mind of Clara had become again active, and measurably calm, she said to her—

"It was a cruel jest, and the consequences have been most painful. But I trust it is not yet too late to repair the wrong thus done, although no compensation can be made for the suffering to which you have been subjected."

"It is too late, Mrs. Mears—too late!" replied Clara, in a mournful voice.

"Say not so, my dear young friend."

But Clara shook her head.

It was in vain that Mrs. Mears strove earnestly to lift up her drooping heart. The calmness with which she had been able to bear the destruction of all her hopes, because there had seemed an adequate cause for the sacrifice she had made, was all gone now. There had been no adequate cause for the sacrifice. Her lover was as excellent and honourable as she at first believed him to be, and she had cast him off on the authority of a heartless jest. To all that her friend could say, she had but one reply to make—

"It is too late now!"

"Not too late, I trust," said Mr. Mears, a good deal disturbed by his wife's relation of her interview with Clara. "I must ascertain where Fisher is, and write to him on the subject. Did she say any thing that led you to believe that she recognised the voices of the persons whom she heard conversing? Do you think she suspects me in the matter?"

"I do not think she does."

"So much the better."

The effect upon Clara of the information she had received was very serious. Deeply as she had been afflicted, the consciousness of having done right in refusing to marry a man who was destitute, as she had accidentally discovered, of virtuous principles, sustained her. But now it was revealed to her that he was as excellent as she had at first believed him, and that she had been made the victim of a pleasant joke! There was no longer any thing to hold her up, and accordingly her spirits completely forsook her, and in less than two weeks she was seriously ill.

The news of this deeply disturbed Mr. Mears, who had written to Fisher, and was waiting impatiently for an answer.

"I am afraid we have made the matter worse," he said to his wife, who, on returning from a visit to Clara, reported that, so far from improving, she was too evidently sinking, daily. "If Fisher should have entered into another engagement, or, if his pride has taken fire at being thrown off on what may appear to him such slight grounds, I really tremble for the consequences."

"Let us hope for the best," returned Mrs. Mears, "as we have acted for the best. It was plainly our duty to do as we have done. On that subject I have no doubt."

Two more weeks of painful suspense and anxiety passed. Clara did not improve in the least. Mrs. Mears called to see her every few days, but dared not venture to tell her that her husband had written to Fisher. She was afraid to fill her mind with this hope, lest it should fail, and the shock prove too severe. But, even as it was, life seemed to be rapidly ebbing away.

At length there came a change. Nature rallied, and life, flowed, though feebly still, in healthier currents through the veins of Clara Grant. In a week from the time this change took place, she was able to leave her bed and set up for a few hours each day. But all who looked into her young face were grieved at the sight. There were no deep lines of distress there, but the marks of patient, yet hopeless suffering.

One day, she sat alone, in a dreamy, musing state, with a book lying upon her lap. She had been trying to read, but found it impossible to take any interest in the pages over which her eyes passed, while her mind scarcely apprehended the sense. Some one opened the door; but she did not look around. The person, whoever it was, remained only for a moment or two, and then withdrew. In a little while the door opened again, and some one entered and came towards her with the tread of a man. She started to her feet, while her heart gave a sudden bound. As she turned, her eyes fell upon the form of her long absent lover. For an instant, perhaps longer, she looked into his face to read it as the index of his heart, and then she lay quivering on his bosom.

A few weeks later, Clara became the bride of Charles Fisher, and left with him for the South. Neither of them ever knew the authors of the wrong they had suffered. It was better, perhaps, that in this they should remain ignorant.

So much "*for the fun of it.*"

FORGIVE AND FORGET.

Forgive and forget! Why the world would be lonely,
The garden a wilderness left to deform,
If the flowers but remembered the chilling winds only,
And the fields gave no verdure for fear of the storm! C.
SWAIN.

"FORGIVE and forget, Herbert."

"No, I will neither forgive nor forget. The thing was done wantonly. I never pass by a direct insult."

"Admit that it was done wantonly; but this I doubt. He is an old friend, long tried and long esteemed. He could not have been himself; he must have been carried away by some wrong impulse, when he offended you."

"He acted from something in him, of course."

"We all do so. Nothing external can touch our volition, unless there be that within which corresponds to the impelling agent."

"Very well. This conduct of Marston shows him to be internally unworthy of my regard; shows him to possess a trait of character that unfits him to be my friend. I have been mistaken in him. He now stands revealed in his true light, a mean-spirited fellow."

"Don't use such language towards Marston, my young friend."

"He has no principle. He wished to render me ridiculous and do me harm. A man who could act as he did, cannot possess a spark of honourable feeling. Does a good fountain send forth bitter waters? Is not a tree known by its fruit? When a man seeks wantonly to insult and injure me, I discover that he wants principle, and wish to have no more to do with him."

"Perhaps," said the individual with whom Herbert Arnest was conversing, "it is your wounded self-love, more than your high regard for principle, that speaks so eloquently against Marston."

"Mr. Welford!"

"Nay, my young friend, do not be offended with me. Your years, twice told, would not make mine. I have lived long enough to get a cool

- 79 -

head and understand something of the springs of action that lie in the human heart. The best, at best, have little to be proud of, and much to lament over, in the matter of high and honourable impulses. It is a far easier thing to do wrong than right; far easier to be led away by our evil passions than to compel ourselves always to regard justice and judgment in our dealings with others. Test yourself by this rule. Would your feelings for Marston be the same if he had only acted toward another as he has acted toward you? Do not say 'yes' from a hasty impulse. Reflect coolly about it. If not, then it is not so much a regard to principle, as your regard to yourself, that causes you to be so bitterly offended."

This plain language was not relished by the young man. It was touching the very thing in him that Marston had offended—his self-love. He replied, coldly—

"As for that, I am very well satisfied with my own reasons for being displeased with Marston; and am perfectly willing to be responsible for my own action in this case. I will change very much from my present feelings, if I ever have any thing more to do with him."

"God give you a better mind then," replied Mr. Welford. "It is the best wish I can express for you."

The two young men who were now at variance with each other had been friends for many years. As they entered the world, the hereditary character of each came more fully into external manifestation, and revealed traits not before seen, and not always the most agreeable to others. Edward Marston had his faults, and so had Herbert Arnest: the latter quite as many as the former. There was a mutual observation of these, and a mutual forbearance towards each other for a considerable time, although each thought more than was necessary about things in the other that ought to be corrected. A fault with Marston was quickness of temper and a disposition to say unpleasant, cutting things, without due reflection. But he had a forgiving disposition, and very many amiable and excellent qualities. Arnest was also quick-tempered. His leading defect of character was self-esteem, which made him exceedingly sensitive in regard to the conduct of others as affecting the general estimation of himself. He could not bear to have any freedom taken with him, in company, even by his best friend. He felt it to be humiliating, if not degrading. He, therefore, was a man of many dislikes, for one and another were every now and then doing or saying something that hurt more or less severely his self-esteem.

Marston had none of this peculiar weakness of his friend. He rarely thought about the estimation in which he was held, and never let the mere opinions of others influence him. But he was careful not to do any thing that violated his own self-respect.

The breach between the young men occurred thus. The two friends were in company with several others, and there was present a young lady in whose eyes Arnest wished to appear in as favourable a light as possible. He was relating an adventure in which he was the principal hero, and, in doing so, exaggerated his own action so far as to amuse Marston, who happened to know all about the circumstances, and provoke from him some remarks that placed the whole affair in rather a ridiculous light, and caused a laugh at Arnest's expense.

The young man's self-esteem was deeply wounded. Even the lady, for whose ears the narrative had been more especially given, laughed heartily, and made one or two light remarks; or, rather, heavy ones for the ears of Arnest. He was deeply disturbed though at the time he managed to conceal almost entirely what he felt.

Marston, however, saw that his thoughtless words had done more (sic) than he had intended them to do, both upon the company and upon the sensitive mind of his friend. He regretted having uttered them and waited only until he should leave the company with Arnest, to express his sorrow for what he had done. But his friend did not give him this opportunity, for he managed to retire alone, thus expressing to Marston the fact that he was seriously offended.

Early the next morning, Marston called at the residence of his friend, in order to make an apology for having offended him; but he happened not to be at home. On arriving at his office, he found a note from Arnest, couched in the most offensive terms. The language was such as to extinguish all desire or intention to apologize.

"Henceforth we are strangers," he said, as he thrust the note aside.

An hour afterward, they met on the street, looked coldly into each other's face, and passed without even a nod. That act sealed the record of estrangement.

Mr. Wellford was an old gentleman who was well acquainted with both of the young men, and esteemed them for the good qualities they possessed. When he heard of the occurrence just related, he was much grieved, and sought to heal the breach that had been made; but without success. Arnest's self-esteem had been sorely wounded, and he would not forgive what he considered a wanton outrage. Marston felt himself deeply insulted by the note he had received, and maintained that he would forfeit his self-respect were he to hold any intercourse whatever with a man who could, on so small a provocation, write such a scandalous letter. Thus the matter stood; wounded self-esteem on one side, and insulted self-respect on the other, not only maintaining the breach, but widening it every day.

Mr Wellford used his utmost influence with his young friends to bend them from their anger, but he argued the matter in vain. The voice of pride was stronger than the voice of reason.

Months were suffered to go by, and even years to elapse, and still they were as strangers. Circumstances threw them constantly together; they met in places of business; they sat in full view of each other in church on the holy Sabbath; they mingled in the same social circles; the friends of one were the friends of the other; but they rarely looked into each other's face, and never spoke. Did this make them happier? No! For, "*If ye forgive not men their trespasses, neither will your heavenly Father forgive your trespasses.*" Did they feel indifferent toward each other? Not by any means! Arnest still dwelt on and magnified the provocation he had received, but thought that the expression of his indignation had not been of a character to give as great offence to Marston as it had done. And Marston, as time passed, thought more and more lightly of the few jesting words he had spoken, and considered them less and less provocation for the insulting note he had received, which he still had, and sometimes turned up and read.

The old friends were forced to think of each other often, for both were rising in the world, and rising into general esteem and respectability. The name of the one was often mentioned with approbation in the presence of the other; and it sometimes happened that they were thrown together in such a way as to render their position toward each other really embarrassing: as, for instance, one was called to preside at a public meeting, and the other chosen secretary. Neither could refuse, and there had to be an official intercourse between them; it was cold and formal in the extreme; and neither could see as he looked into the eyes of the other, a glimmer of the old light of friendship.

Mr. Wellford was present at this meeting, and marked the fact that the intercourse between Arnest and Marston was official only—that they did not unbend to each other in the least. He was grieved to see it, for he knew the good qualities of both, and he had a high respect for them.

"This must not be," said he to himself, as he walked thoughtfully homeward. "They are making themselves unhappy, and preventing a concert of useful efforts for good in society, and all for nothing. I will try again to reconcile them; perhaps I may be more successful than before."

So, on the next day, the old gentleman made it his business to call upon Arnest, who expressed great pleasure in meeting him.

"I noticed," said Mr. Wellford, after he had conversed some time, and finally introduced the subject of the meeting on the previous evening, "that your intercourse with the secretary was exceedingly formal; in fact, hardly courteous."

"I don't like Marston, as you are very well aware," replied Arnest.

"In which feeling you stand nearly alone, friend Arnest. Mr. Marston is highly esteemed by all who know him."

"All don't know him as I do."

"Perhaps others know him better than you do; there may lie the difference."

"If a man knocks me down, I know the weight of his arm much better than those who have never felt it."

"Still nursing your anger, still harbouring unkind thoughts! Forgive and forget, my friend—forgive and forget; no longer let the sun go down upon your wrath."

"I can forgive, Mr. Wellford—I do forgive; for Heaven knows I wish him no harm; but I cannot forget: that is asking too much."

"You do not forget, because you will not forgive," replied the old gentleman. "Forgive, and you will soon forget. I am sure you will both be happier in forgetting than you can be in remembering the past."

But Arnest shook his head, remarking, as he so—"I would rather let things remain as they are. At least, I cannot stoop to any humiliating overtures for a reconciliation. When Marston outraged my feelings so wantonly, I wrote him a pretty warm expression of my sentiments in regard to his conduct. This gave him mortal offence. I do not now remember what I wrote, but nothing, certainly, to have prevented his coming forward and apologizing for his conduct; but he did not choose to do this, and there the matter rests. I cannot recall the angry rebuke I gave him, for it was no doubt just."

"A man who writes a letter in a passion, and afterwards forgets what he has written," said Mr. Wellford, "may be sure that he has said what his sober reason cannot approve. If you could have the letter you then sent before you now, I imagine that you would no longer wonder that Marston was offended."

"That is impossible; without doubt, he burned my note the moment he received it."

Mr. Wellford tried in vain to induce Arnest to consent to forget what was past; but he affirmed that this was impossible, and that he had no wish to renew an acquaintance with his old friend.

About the same time that this interview took place, Marston was alone, thinking with sad and softened feelings of the past. The letter of Arnest was before him; he had turned it over by accident.

"He could not have been himself when he wrote this," he thought. It was the first time he had permitted himself to think so. "My words must have stung him severely, lightly as I uttered them, and with no intention to wound. This matter ought not to have gone on so long. Friends are not so plentiful that we may carelessly cast those we have tried and proved aside. He has many excellent qualities."

Pride came quickly, with many suggestions about self-respect, and what every man owed to himself.

"He owes it to himself to be just to others," Marston truly thought. "Was I just in failing to apologize to my friend, notwithstanding this offensive letter? No, I was not; for his action did not exonerate me from the responsibility of mine. Ah, me! How passion blinds us!"

After musing for some time, Marston drew towards him a sheet of paper, and, taking up a pen, wrote:

> "MY DEAR SIR:—What I ought to have
> done years ago, I do now, and that is, offer
> you a sincere apology for light words
> thoughtlessly spoken, but which I ought not to
> have used, as they were calculated to wound,
> and, I am grieved to think, did wound. But for
> your note, which I enclose, I should have
> made this apology the moment I had an
> opportunity. But its peculiar tenor, I then felt,
> precluded me from doing so. I confess that I
> erred in letting my feelings blind my cooler
> judgment.

> "Your old friend, MARSTON.

> "To Mr. Herbert Arnest."

Enclosing the note alluded to in this letter, Marston sealed, and, ringing for an attendant, despatched it.

"Better to do right late than never," he murmured, as he leaned pensively back in his chair.

"Let what will come of it, I shall feel better, for I will gain my own self-respect, and have an inward assurance that I have done right,—more than I have for a long time had, in regard to this matter at least."

Relieved in mind, Marston commenced looking over some papers in reference to matters of business then on hand, and was soon so much absorbed in them, that the subject which had lately filled his thoughts faded entirely therefrom. Some one opened the door, and he turned to see who was entering. In an instant he was on his feet. It was Arnest.

The face of the latter was pale and agitated, and his lips quivered. He came forward hurriedly, extending his hand, not to grasp that of his old friend, but to hold up his own letter that had been just returned to him.

"Marston," he said, huskily, "did I send you *this* note?"

"You did," was the firm but mild answer.

"Thus I cancel it!" And he tore it into shreds, and scattered them on the floor. "Would that its contents could be as easily obliterated from your memory!" he added, in a most earnest voice.

"They are no longer there, my friend," returned Marston, with visible emotion, now grasping the hand of Arnest. "You have wiped them out."

Arnest returned the pressure with both hands, his eyes fixed on those of Marston, until they grew so dim that he could no longer read the old familiar lines and forgiving look.

"Let us forgive and forget," said Marston, speaking in a broken voice. "We have wronged each other and ourselves. We have let evil passions rule instead of good affections."

"From my heart do I say 'Amen,'" replied Arnest. "Yes, let us forgive and forget. Would that we had been as wise as we now are, years ago!"

Thus were they reconciled. And now the question is, What did either gain by his indignation against the other? Did Arnest rise higher in his self-esteem, or Marston gain additional self-respect? We think not. Alas! how blinding is selfish passion! How it opens in the mind the door for the influx of multitudes of evil and false suggestions! How it hides the good in others, and magnifies, weakness into crimes! Let us beware of it.

"Reconciled at last," said old Mr. Wellford, when he next saw Arnest and heard the fact from his lips.

"Yes," replied the latter. "I can now forget as well as forgive."

"Rather say you can forget, *because* you forgive. If you had forgiven truly, you could have ceased to think of what was wrong in your friend long ago. People talk of forgiving and not forgetting, but it isn't so: they do not forget because they do not forgive."

"I believe you are right," said Arnest. "I think, now, as naturally of my friend's good qualities as I ever did before of what was evil. I forget the evil in thinking of the good."

"Because you have forgiven him," returned Mr. Wellford. "Before you forgave him, your thought of evil gave no room for the thought of good."

Mr. Wellford was right. After we have forgiven, we find it no hard matter to forget.

PAYING THE MINISTER.

"MONEY, money, money! That's the everlasting cry! I'll give up my pew. I won't go to church. I'll stay at home and read the Bible. Not that I care for a few dollars more than I do for the dust that blows in the wind; but this selling of salvation for gold disgusts me. I'm sick to death of it!"

"But hear, first, Mr. Larkin, what we want money for," said Mr. Elder, one of the vestrymen of the church to which the former belonged. "You know that our minister's salary is very small; in fact, entirely insufficient for the maintenance of his family. He has, as might be supposed, fallen into debt, and we are making an effort to raise a sufficient sum to relieve him from his unpleasant embarrassment."

"But what business has he to go in debt, Mr. Elder? He knows the amount of his income, and, as an honest man, should not let his expenses exceed it."

"But you know as well as I do that he cannot live on four hundred dollars a year."

"I don't know any such thing, friend Elder. But I do know, that there are hundreds and thousands who live on much less, and save a little into the bargain. That, however, is neither here nor there. Four hundred dollars a year is all this parish can afford to pay a minister, and that Mr. Malcolm was distinctly told before he came. If he could not live on the salary offered, why did he come? Mr. Pelton never received more."

"Beg your pardon, Mr. Larkin. Mr. Pelton never received less than seven hundred dollars a year. There were always extra subscriptions made for him."

"I never gave any thing more than my regular subscription and pew-rent."

"It is more than I can say, then. In presents of one kind and another and in money it never cost me less than from fifty to seventy-five dollars a year extra. Having been in the vestry for the last ten years, I happen to know that there was always something to make up at the end of the year, and it generally came out of the pockets of a few."

"Well, it isn't right, that is all I have to say," returned Mr. Larkin. "A minister has no business to saddle himself upon a congregation in that way for less than his real weight. It's an imposition, and one that I am not going to stand. I'm opposed to all these forced levies, from principle."

"I rather think the first error is on the side of the congregation," said Mr. Elder. "I think they are not only to blame, but really dishonest, in fixing upon a sum for the support of a minister that is plainly inadequate to his maintenance. Here, in our parish, for instance, a thousand dollars might be paid to a minister with the greatest ease in the world, and no one be oppressed by his subscription. And yet, we are very content and self-complacent in our niggardly tender of four hundred dollars."

"A thousand dollars! I don't believe any minister ought to receive such a salary. I have no notion of tempting, by inducements like that, money-lovers into the sacred office."

"Pardon me, Mr. Larkin, but how much does it cost you to live? Not less than two thousand five hundred dollars a year, I presume."

"But I don't put my expenses alongside of the minister's. I can afford to spend all that it costs me. I have honestly made what I possess, and have a right to enjoy it."

"I didn't question that, Mr. Larkin. I only turned your thoughts in this direction, that you might realize in your own mind how hard it must be for a man with a family of three children, just the number that you have, to live on four hundred dollars a year."

But the allusion to matters personal to Mr. Larkin gave that gentleman a fine opportunity to feel offended; which he did not fail to embrace, and thus close the interview.

This was Mr. Elder's first effort to obtain a subscription for paying off the minister's debt. It quite disheartened him. He had intended making three calls on his way to his store that morning, for the purpose of trying to raise something for Mr. Malcolm; but he felt so discouraged by the reception he had met with from Mr. Larkin, that he passed on without doing so. Near his store was a carriage repository. The owner of it put his hand upon his shoulder as he was going by, and said, "Just step in, I want to show you something beautiful."

Mr. Elder went in, and was shown a very handsome and fashionably-made carriage, with all the modern improvements.

"This is something very elegant, certainly. Who is it for?"

"One of the members of your church."

"Ah?"

"Yes. It is for Larkin."

"Indeed! How much does it cost him?"

"Eight hundred dollars."

"He ought to have a fine pair of horses for so fine a carriage."

"And so he has. He bought a noble span, last week, for a thousand dollars."

Mr. Elder said what he could in praise of the elegant carriage; but he couldn't say much, for he had no heart to do so. He felt worse than ever about the deficiency in Mr. Malcolm's salary. On the next day he was in better spirits, and called in upon one of the members of the church, as he passed to his store. He stated his errand, and received this reply—

"I'll tell you what, Mr. Elder, I am of Larkin's opinion in this matter. If our minister agreed to come for four hundred dollars, he should stick to his contract. He's no business to go in debt, and then call upon us to get him out of his difficulties. It isn't the clean thing. I don't mind a few dollars any more than you do; but I like principle. I like to see all men, especially ministers, stick to their text. Malcolm knew before he came here what we could afford to give him, and if he couldn't live upon that, he had no business to come. That's what I think of it, and I always speak out my mind plainly."

Mr. Elder made no more begging calls on that day. But he tried it again on the next, and found that Larkin had been over the ground before him, and said so much about "the imposition of the thing," that he could do little or nothing. There was a speciousness about Larkin's manner of alluding to the subject, that carried people away with him; particularly as what he said favoured their inclination to keep a tight hold on their purse-strings. He was piqued with Elder, and this set him to talking, and doing more mischief than he thought for.

The Rev. Mr. Malcolm was a man of about thirty years of age. He had taken orders a couple of years previous to the date of his call to the parish where he now preached. At the time of doing so, he was engaged in teaching a school; from which he received a very comfortable income. The bishop who ordained him recommended the parish at C—, when Mr. Pelton left there, to apply for Mr. Malcolm; which was done. The latter was an honest, conscientious man, and sincere in his desire to do good in the sacred office to which he believed himself called. When the invitation to settle at C— came, he left home and visited the parish, in order that he might determine whether it was his duty to go there or not. On his return, his wife inquired, with a good deal of interest, how he liked the place, and if he thought he would go there.

"I think I shall accept the call," said he. This was not spoken with much warmth.

"Don't you like the people?" inquired Mrs. Malcolm.

"Yes; as far as I saw them, they were very pleasant, good sort of people. But the salary is entirely too small."

"How much?"

"Four hundred dollars a year, and the parsonage—a little affair, that would rent for about a hundred dollars."

"We can't live on that," said Mrs. Malcolm, in a disappointed tone; "it is out of the question."

"No, certainly not. But I am assured that at least seven or eight hundred will be made up during the year. This has always been done for Mr. Pelton and will be done for me, if I accept the call."

"That might do, if we practised close economy. But why do they not make the salary seven or eight hundred dollars at once? It would be just the same to them, and make the minister feel a great deal more independent."

"True; but we must let people do things in their own way. We can live on seven hundred dollars, and I therefore think it my duty to give up my school, and accept the call."

"No one, certainly, can charge you with sordid views in doing so, for your school yields you now over a thousand dollars, and is increasing."

"I will try and keep my mind free from all thought of what people may say or think," returned Mr. Malcolm, "and endeavour to do right for the sake of right."

The wife of the Rev. Mr. Malcolm fully sympathized with her husband in his wish to enter upon the duties of his sacred calling, and was ready to make any sacrifice that could be made in order to see him in the position he so much desired to occupy. She did not, therefore, make any objection to giving up their pleasant home and sufficient income, but went with him cheerfully to C—, and there made every effort to reduce all their expenses to their reduced means of living.

It is a much easier thing to increase our expenses than to reduce them. We get used to a certain free way of living, and it is one of the most difficult things in the world to give up this little luxury, and that pleasant indulgence, and come right down to the meagre necessaries of life. This fact was soon apparent to Mr. and Mrs. Malcolm; but they were in earnest in what they were about, and practised the required self-denial. Their expenses were kept within the limits of seven hundred dollars, the lowest sum that had been named.

At the end of the first three months, one hundred dollars were paid to the minister. When he gave up his school, he sold it out to a person who wished to succeed him, for two hundred dollars. The expense of removing to C—, and living there for three months, had quite exhausted this sum. Mr. Malcolm paid away his last dollar before the quarter's salary was due, and was forced to let his bread-bill and his meat-bill run on for a couple of weeks; these were paid the moment he received his salary.

"I don't like these bills at all," said he to his wife, after they were paid. "A minister should never owe a dollar; it does him no good. Above all things, his mind should live in a region above the anxieties that a deficient income and consequent debt always occasion. We must husband what we have, and make it go as far as possible."

By the end of two months, the hundred dollars were all expended; but not a word had been said about the additional three or four hundred that had been promised, or that Mr. Malcolm fully believed had been promised. Bills had now to be run up with the baker, grocer, and butcher, which amounted to nearly fifty dollars when the next quarter's salary was paid.

Mr. Malcolm did not doubt but the additional amount promised when he consented to accept the call would be made up; still he could not help feeling troubled. If things went on as they were going, by the end of the year he would be in debt at least two hundred dollars; and, of all things in the world, he had a horror of debt.

During this time, he was in familiar intercourse with the principal members of his church, and especially with the leading vestrymen who held out inducements to him beyond the fixed salary; but no allusion was made to the subject, and he had too much delicacy to introduce it.

At last, matters approached a climax. The minister was about two hundred dollars in debt, and bills were presented almost every week, and their settlement politely urged. This was a condition of things not to be endured by a man of Mr. Malcolm's high sense of right and peculiar delicacy of feeling. At length, after lying awake for half of the night, thinking over what was to be done, he came to the reluctant conclusion that it was his imperative duty to those he owed, to mention the necessities of his case to the vestry, and learn from them, without further delay, whether he had any thing beyond the four hundred dollars to expect.

The hardest task Mr. Malcolm had ever performed was now before him, and he shrunk from it with painful reluctance. But the path of duty was plain, and he was not a man to hold back when he saw his way clear. If there had been any hesitation, an imperative dun received before he sat down to breakfast, and another before nine o'clock, would have effectually dispelled it.

Mr. Malcolm went to the store of Mr. Elder, one of the vestrymen, and found him quite busy with customers. He waited for half an hour for him to be disengaged, and then went out, saying, as he passed him at the counter, that he would call in again.

"Oh, dear!" he murmured to himself, with a long-drawn sigh, as he emerged upon the street, "is not this humiliating? If I had engaged for only four hundred dollars a year, I would have lived on bread and water rather than have exceeded my income; but at least seven hundred were promised. It was, however, an informal promise; and I was wrong, perhaps, in trusting to any thing so unsettled as this. Of course, it will be paid to me when I make known my present situation; but the doing of that I shrink from."

"Mr. T— was here again for his bill," were the first words that saluted the ears of the minister when he returned home.

"What did you say to him?" he asked.

"I told him that you would settle it very soon. He said he hoped you would, for he wanted money badly, and it had been running for some time."

"He was rude, then!"

"A little so," replied the wife, in a meek voice.

Mr. Malcolm paced the floor with rapid steps; he felt deeply disturbed.

An hour afterwards, he entered the store of Mr. Elder, and found the owner disengaged. He did not linger in preliminaries, but approached the subject thus:—

"You remember, Mr. Elder, that in the interview I had with you and two of the vestry previous to my accepting the call of this parish, you stated that my income would not be limited to the four hundred dollars named as the minister's salary, which I then told you was a smaller sum than I could possibly live upon?"

Mr. Elder exhibited a momentary confusion when the minister said this; but he immediately replied—"Yes, I believe something was said on that subject, though I have not thought of it since. We always had to make up something for Mr. Pelton, and I suppose we must do the same for you, if it is necessary. Do you find your salary inadequate?"

"Entirely so; and I knew it would be inadequate from the first. It is impossible for me to support my family on four hundred dollars; and had I not been assured that at least three or four hundred dollars extra would be made up during the year, I never would have dreamed of accepting the call. It has been a principle with me not to go in debt; and since I have been a man, I have not, until this time, owed a dollar; and should not have owed it now, had I received, since I have resided in C— the income I fully expected."

Mr. Malcolm spoke with warmth, for he felt some risings of the natural man at the indifference with which a promise of so much consequence to him had been disregarded.

"How much do you owe?" inquired the vestryman.

"About two hundred dollars."

"Indeed! so much?"

A bitter remark arose to the minister's lips, but he forced himself to keep silence. He was a man, with all the natural feelings of a man.

"Well, I suppose we must make it for you somehow," said Mr. Elder, the tone in which he spoke showing that the subject worried him. "Are any of the demands on you pressing?" he inquired, after a pause.

"All of them are pressing," replied the minister. "I am dunned every day."

"Indeed! That's bad!" returned Mr. Elder, speaking with more real kindness and sympathy than at first. "I am sorry you have been permitted to get into so unpleasant a situation."

"It certainly is very unpleasant, and entirely destroys my peace. Were I not thus unhappily situated, I should not have said a word to you on the subject of my salary."

"Don't let it distress you so much, Mr. Malcolm. I will see that the amount you need is at once made up."

The minister returned home, disturbed, mortified, and humiliated.

"If this is the way they pay their minister," he remarked to his wife, after relating to her what had happened, "it is the last year that I shall enjoy the benefits of their peculiar system. But little good will my preaching or that of any one else do them, while they disregard the first and plainest principles of honesty. There is no lack of ability to give a minister the support he needs; and the withholding of that support, or the supplying of it by constraint, shows a moral obtuseness that argues but poorly for their love of any thing but themselves. I believe that the labourer is worthy of his hire; that when men build a church and call a minister for their own spiritual good, they are bound to supply his natural wants; and that, if they fail to do so, it is a sign to the minister that he ought to leave them. Some may call this a selfish doctrine, and unworthy of a minister of God; but I believe it to be the true doctrine, and shall act up to it. It does men no good to let them quietly go on, year after year, starving their ministers, while they have abundant means to make them comfortable. If they prize their wealth higher than they do spiritual riches, it is but casting pearls before swine to scatter even the most brilliant gems of wisdom before them; and in this unprofitable task I am the last man to engage. I gave up all hope of worldly good, in order to preach the everlasting gospel for the salvation of men. In order to do this successfully, my mind must be kept free from the depressing cares of life, and there must be something reciprocal in those to whom I minister in heavenly things. If this be not the case, all my labour will be in vain."

On the next day, as the minister was walking down the street, he met Mr. Larkin. The allusion to this gentleman's personal matters, which the vestryman had made, still caused him to feel sore; it touched him in a vulnerable part. He had been talking quite freely, since then, to every member of the church he happened to meet about the coolness with which Mr. Malcolm, after running himself in debt, a thing he had no business to do, called upon the church to raise him more money. He for one he said, was not going to stand any such nonsense, and he hoped every member of the church would as firmly set his face against all such impositions. If they were to pay off this debt, they would have another twice as large to settle in a few months. It was the principle of the thing he went against; not that he cared about a few dollars. As soon as Mr. Larkin saw the minister a little ahead of him, he determined to give him a piece of his mind. So when they paused, face to face, and while their hands were locked in a friendly clasp, he said—

"Look here, friend Malcolm, I have got something against you; and as I am an independent plain-spoken man, you must not be offended with me for telling you my mind freely."

"The truth never offends me, Mr. Larkin," said the minister, with a smile. "I am not faultless, though willing to correct my faults when I see them."

"Very well." Mr. Larkin spoke in a resolute voice, and seemed to feel pleasure rather than pain in what he was doing. "In the first place, then, I am sorry to find that you possess one very bad fault, common to most ministers, and that is, a disposition to live beyond your means, and then come down upon the parish to pay your debts."

The blood came rushing to the face of the minister, which his monitor took to be the plainest kind of evidence that he had hit the nail fully upon the head. He went on more confidently.

"Now, this, Mr. Malcolm, I consider to be very wrong—very wrong, indeed!—and especially so in a young minister in his first year, and in his first parish. If such things are in the green tree, what are we to expect in the dry? You accepted our call, and were plainly informed that the salary would be four hundred dollars and rent free. Upon this our former minister had lived quite comfortably. If you thought the salary too little, you should not have accepted the call—accepting it, you should have lived upon it, if you had lived on bread and water."

Mr. Larkin paused. The minister stood with his eyes cast upon the pavement, but made no answer. Mr. Larkin resumed—

"It is such things as this that bring scandal upon the church, and drive right thinking men out of it. It isn't that I value a few dollars more than I do the wind; but I like to see principle; and hate all imposition. You are a young man, Mr. Malcolm, and I speak thus plainly to you for your good. I hope you will not feel offended."

Mr. Larkin paused, thinking, perhaps, that he had said enough. The minister's eyes were still upon the pavement, from which he lifted them as soon as his monitor was done speaking. The flush had left his cheeks, that were now pale.

"I thank you for your honesty in speaking so plainly, and will try to profit by what you have told me," said he, calmly. "The best of us are liable to err."

There was something in the words, voice, and manner of the minister that Mr. Larkin did not clearly comprehend. He had spoken harshly, and, he now felt, with some rudeness; but, while there was nothing in the air with which his reproof was received that evidenced the conviction of error there was no resentment. A moment before, he felt like a superior severely reprimanding an inferior; but now he stood in the presence of one whose calmness and dignity oppressed him. He was about commencing a confused apology for his apparent harshness, when Mr. Malcolm bowed and passed on.

Larkin did not feel very comfortable as he walked away. He soon more than half repented of what he had done, and before night, by way of atonement for his error, called upon Mr. Elder, and handed him a check for twenty-five dollars, to help pay off the minister's debt. So much for the principle concerned.

On the next Sabbath, to his great surprise, when the text was announced, it was in the following unexpected words—

"Owe no man any thing."

The sermon was didactive and narrative. In the didactic portion, the minister was exceedingly close in laying down the principles of honesty in all transactions between man and man, and showed that for a man to live beyond his known income, when that was sufficient to supply his actual wants, was dishonest. Then he gave sundry examples of very common but dishonest practices in those who withhold from others what is justly their due, and concluded this portion of his discourse, by plainly stating the glaring dishonesty of which too many congregations were guilty, in owing their ministers the difference between their regular and fixed income, and what they actually needed for their comfortable support and freedom from care. This, he said, was but a poor commentary upon their love for the church, and showed too plainly its sordid and selfish quality.

This was felt by many to be quite too pointed and out of place; and for a young man, like him, very bold and immodest. One member took out his box and struck the lid a smart, emphatic rap before taking a pinch of snuff,—another coughed—and three or four of the older ones gave several loud "a-h-h-hems!" Throughout the church there was an uneasy movement. But soon all was still again, for the minister had commenced the narrative of something which he said had occurred in a parish at no great distance. For a narrative, introduced in a sermon, all ears are open.

Very deliberately and very minutely did Mr. Malcolm give the leading facts which we have already placed before the reader, even down to the sound lecture he had received from Mr. Larkin, and then closed his sermon, after a few words of application, with a firm repetition of his text:

"My brethren, 'Owe no man any thing.'"

Of course, there was a buzzing in the hive after this. One made inquiries of another, and it was soon pretty well understood throughout, that seven or eight hundred dollars had actually been promised to the minister instead of the four, which all were very content that he should receive, thinking little and caring little whether he lived well or ill upon it. But who was it that had rated him so soundly? That was the next question. But nobody knew. Some of those most familiar with Mr. Malcolm boldly asked him the question, but he declined giving an answer. Poor Mr. Larkin trembled but the minister kept his own counsel.

On the Tuesday following this pointed discourse, Mr. Malcolm received his last quarter's salary four weeks in advance, and three hundred dollars besides. Two hundred of this had been loaned by Mr. Larkin until such time as it could be collected.

At the next meeting of the vestry, the resignation of Mr. Malcolm as minister of the parish was received. Before acting upon it, a church-meeting was called, at which it was unanimously voted to double the ministers salary. That is, make it eight hundred. Much was said in his favour as a man of fine talents and sincere piety. In fact, the congregation generally had become much attached to him, and could not bear to think of his leaving them. Money was no consideration now.

The vote of the meeting was conveyed to Mr. Malcolm. He expressed his thanks for the liberal offer, but again declined remaining. Another church-meeting was called, and a thousand dollars unhesitatingly named as the minister's salary, if he would stay. Many doubled their subscriptions, and said that, if necessary, they would quadruple them.

When Mr. Malcolm determined to leave C—, he had no parish in view; but he did not think it would be useful for him to remain. Nor had he any in view when he declined accepting the offer of eight hundred dollars. But it was different when the offer of a thousand dollars came, for then he held in his hand a call to a neighbouring parish, where the salary was the same.

The committee to wait upon him, and urge him to accept the still better terms offered, was composed of Messrs. Elder, Larkin, and three others among the oldest and most influential members. He answered their renewed application by handing them the letter he had just received. It was read aloud.

"If money is any object, Mr. Malcolm," said Larkin, promptly, "you need not leave us. Twelve hundred can be as easily made up to you as a thousand."

The minister was slightly disturbed at this. He replied in a low, unsteady voice:

"Money has no influence with me in this matter. All I ask is a comfortable maintenance for my family. This, your first offer of eight hundred dollars would have given; but I declined it, with no other place in view, because I thought it best for both you and me that we should separate. I have tried only to look to the good of the church in my decisions, and I will still endeavour to keep that end before my eyes."

"Have you accepted the call?" asked Mr. Elder.

"No, I have but just received it!"

"Have you positively determined that you will not remain with us?"

"I should not like to say positively."

"Very well. Now, let me say that the desire to have you remain is general, and that the few who have the management of the church affairs, and not the many who make up the congregation, are to blame for previously existing wrongs and errors. From the many comes a strong desire to have you stay. They say that your ministrations have been of great spiritual benefit to them, and that if you go away, they will suffer loss. Under these circumstances, Mr. Malcolm, are you willing to break your present connection?"

"Give me a few hours to reflect," replied the minister, a good deal affected by this unlooked-for appeal. "I wish to do right; and in doing it, am ready to cut off the right hand and pluck out the right eye. As Heaven is my witness, I set before me no earthly reward. If I do consent to remain, I will not receive more than your first offer of eight hundred dollars, for on that I can live comfortably."

When the committee again waited on Mr. Malcolm, to receive his answer, it was in the affirmative; but he was decided in his resolution not to receive more than eight hundred dollars. But the congregation was just as much decided on the other side, and although only two hundred dollars a quarter were paid to their minister by the treasurer, more than fifty dollars flowed in to him during the same period in presents of one useful thing and another, from friends known and unknown.

The parish of C— had quite reformed its mode of paying the minister.

HAD I BEEN CONSULTED.

"HE'S too independent for me," said Matthew Page. "Too independent by half. Had I been consulted he would have done things very differently. But as it is, he will drive his head against the wall before he knows where he is."

"Why don't you advise him to act differently?"

"Advise him, indeed! Oh, no—let him go on in his own way, as he's so fond of it. Young men now-a-days think they know every thing. The experience of men like me goes for nothing with them. Advise him! He may go to the dogs; but he'll get no advice from me unasked."

"You really think he will ruin himself if he goes on in the way he is now going?"

"I know it. Simple addition will determine that, in five minutes. In the first place, instead of consulting me, or some one who knows all about it, he goes and buys that mill for just double what it is worth, and on the mere representation of a stranger, who had been himself deceived, and had an interest in misleading him, in order to get a bad bargain off of his hands. But that is just like your young chaps, now-a-days. They know every thing, and go ahead without talking to anybody. I could have told him, had he consulted me, that, instead of making money by the concern, he would sink all he had in less than two years."

"He is sanguine as to the result."

"I know. He told me, yesterday, that he expected not only to clear his land for nothing, but to make two or three thousand dollars a year out of the lumber for the next ten years. Preposterous!"

"Why didn't you disabuse him of his error, Mr. Page? It was such a good opportunity."

"Let him ask for my advice, if he wants it. It's a commodity I never throw away."

"You might save him from the loss of his little patrimony."

"He deserves to lose it for being such a fool. Buy a steam saw-mill two miles from his land, and expect to make money by clearing it? Ridiculous!"

"Your age and experience will give your advice weight with him, I am sure, Mr. Page. I really think you ought to give a word or two of warning, at least, and thus make an effort to prevent his running through with what little he has. A capital to start with in the world is not so easily obtained, and it is a pity to see Jordan waste his as he is doing."

"No, sir," replied Page. "I shall have nothing to say to him. If he wants my opinion, and asks for it, he shall have it in welcome; not without."

The individuals about whom these persons were conversing was a young man named Jordan, who, at majority, came into the possession of fifty acres of land and about six thousand dollars. The land was still in forest and lay about two miles from a flourishing town in the West, which stood on the bank of a small river that emptied into the Ohio some fifty miles below.

As soon as Jordan became the possessor of the property, he began to turn his thoughts toward its improvement, in order to increase its value. The land did not lie contiguous to his native town, but near to S—, where he was a stranger. To S—he went, and staying at one of the hotels, met with a very pleasant old gentleman who had just built a steam saw-mill on the banks of the river, and was getting in the engine preparatory to putting it in operation. This man's name was Barnaby. He had conceived the idea that a steam saw-mill at that point would be a fortune to any one, and had proceeded to the erection of one forthwith. Logs were to be cut some miles up the river and floated down to the mill, and, after being there manufactured into lumber, to be rafted to a market somewhere between that and New Orleans. Mr. Barnaby had put the whole thing down upon paper, and saw at a glance that it was an operation in which any man's fortune was certain. But, before his mill was completed, he had good reason to doubt the success of his new scheme. He had become acquainted with Matthew Page, a shrewd old resident of S—, who satisfied him, after two or three interviews, that, instead of making a fortune, he would stand a fair chance of losing his whole investment.

Barnaby was about as well satisfied as he wished to be on this head, when young Jordan arrived in S—. His business there was soon known, and Barnaby saw a chance of getting out of his unpromising speculation. To Jordan he became at once very attentive and polite; and gradually drew from him a full statement of the business that brought him to S—. It did not take a very long time for Barnaby to satisfy him, that, by purchasing his mill and sawing up the heavy timber with which his land was covered, he would make a great deal of money, and double the price of his land at the same time. Figures showed the whole result as plain as daylight, and Jordan saw it written out before him as distinctly as he ever saw in his multiplication table that two and two are four. The fairness of Barnaby he did not think of doubting for an instant. His age, address, intelligence, and asseveration of strict honour in every transaction in life, were enough to win his entire confidence.

Five thousand dollars was the price of the mill. The terms upon which it was offered to Jordan were, three thousand dollars in cash, a thousand in six months, and the balance in twelve months.

Shortly after Jordan arrived in the village, he became acquainted with Mr. Page into whose family, a very pleasant one, he had been introduced by a friend. For the old gentleman he felt a good deal of respect; and although it did not occur to him to consult him in regard to his business, thinking that he understood what he was about very well, yet, if Mr. Page had volunteered a suggestion, he would have listened to it and made it the subject of reflection. In fact, a single seriously expressed doubt as to the safety of the investment he was about making, coming from a man like Mr. Page, would have effectually prevented its being made, for Jordan would not have rested until he understood the very nature and groundwork of the objection. He would then have seen a new statement of figures, heard a new relation of facts and probabilities, and learned that Barnaby was selling at the suggestion of Mr. Page, after being fully convinced of the folly of proceeding another step.

But no warning came. The self-esteem of old Matthew Page, who felt himself to be something of an oracle in S—, was touched, because the young man had not consulted him; and now he might go to the dogs, for all he cared.

The preliminaries of sale were soon arranged. Jordan was as eager to enter upon his money-making as Barnaby was to get rid of his money-losing scheme. Three thousand dollars cash were paid, and notes given for the balance. An overseer, or manager of the whole business to be entered upon, was engaged at five hundred dollars a year; some twenty hands to cut timber, haul it to the mill, and saw it up when there, were hired; and twenty yokes of oxen bought for the purpose of hauling the logs from the woods, a distance of two miles. The price of a dollar a log, which Barnaby expected to pay for timber floated down the river, had been considered so dear a rate as to preclude all hope of profit in the business. The great advantages which Jordan felt that he possessed was in himself owning the timber, which had only to be cut and taken to the mill. He had, strangely enough, forgotten to make a calculation of what each log would cost him to cut and haul two miles. There were the wood-choppers at a dollar a day, the teamsters at seventy-five cents a day, and four pairs of oxen to each log to feed. Eight logs a day he was told that each team would haul, and he believed it. But two or three logs were the utmost that could be accomplished, for in the whole distance there was not a quarter of a mile of good solid road.

Six months in time, and a thousand dollars in money, over and above wages to his men, were spent in getting the mill into running order. Jordan had bought under the representation that it was all ready for starting. After he had got in possession, he learned that Barnaby had tried, but in vain, to get the mill to work.

In the mean time, the young man was extending his circle of acquaintance among the families of the place in most of which he was well received and well liked. Old Matthew Page had an only daughter, a beautiful young girl, who was the pride of the village. The first time she and Jordan met, they took a fancy to each other. But as Jordan was rather a modest young man, he did not make very bold advances toward the maiden, although he felt as if he should like to do so, were there any hope of his advances being met in a right spirit.

At the end of a year, all the young man's money was gone, and his last note to Barnaby was due. There was a small pile of lumber by his mill—a couple of hundred dollars worth, perhaps—for which he had found no sale, as the place was fully supplied, and had been for years, by a small mill that was worked by the owner with great economy. The sending of his lumber down the river was rather a serious operation for him, and required a good deal more lumber than he had yet been able to procure from his mill, which had never yet run for twenty-four hours without something getting wrong. These two or three hundred dollars' worth of lumber had cost him about fifteen hundred dollars in wages, &c. Still he was sanguine, and saw his way clear through the whole of it, if it were not for the fact that his capital were exhausted.

Matthew Page was looking on very coolly, and saying to himself, "If he had consulted me," but not offering the young man a word of voluntary counsel.

To continue his operations and bring out the ultimate prosperous result, Jordan threw one-half of his land into market and forced the sale at five dollars an acre. The proceeds of this sale did not last him over six months. Then he got a raft afloat, containing about a thousand dollars' worth of lumber, and sent it off under charge of his overseer, who sold it at Cincinnati, and absconded with the money.

In the mean time, Barnaby was pressing for the payment of the last note, which had been protested, and after threatening to sue, time after time, finally put his claim into the hands of an attorney, who had a writ served upon Jordan.

By this time, old Mr. Page began to think it best, even though not consulted, to volunteer a little advice to the young man. The reason of this may be inferred. Jordan was beginning to be rather particular in attention to Edith, his daughter; and apart from the fact that he had wasted his money in an unprofitable scheme, and had not been prudent enough to consult him, old Matthew Page had no particular objection to him as a son-in-law. His family stood high in the State, and his father, previous to his death, had been for many years in the State senate. The idea that Jordan would take a fancy to his daughter had not once crossed the mind of Mr. Page, or he would not have stood so firmly upon his dignity in the matter of being consulted.

Rather doubting as to the reception he should meet from the young man, he called upon him, one day, when the following conversation took place:

"I'm afraid, Mr. Jordan," said Page, after some commonplace chitchat, "that your saw-mill business is not going to turn out as well as you expected."

"It has not, so far, certainly," replied Jordan, frankly. "But this is owing to the fact of my having been deceived in the mill, and in the integrity of my manager; not to the nature of the business itself. I am still sanguine of success."

"Will you allow me to make a suggestion or two? I think I can show you that you are in error in regard to the business itself."

"Most gladly will I receive any suggestion," returned Jordan. "Though I am not apt to seek advice—a fault of character, perhaps—I am ever ready to listen to it and weigh it dispassionately, when given. A doubt as to the result of the business, if properly carried out, has never yet crossed my mind."

"I have always doubted it from the first. Indeed, I knew that you could not succeed."

"Then, my dear sir, why did you not tell me so?" said Jordan, earnestly.

"If you had consulted me, I would"—

"I never dreamed of consulting any one about it. I had confidence in Mr. Barnaby's statements; but more in my own judgment, based upon the data he furnished me."

"But I have none in either Barnaby or his data."

"I have none in him, for he has shamefully deceived me; but his data are fixed facts, and therefore cannot lie."

"There you err again. Barnaby knew that the data he gave you was incorrect. I had, myself, demonstrated this to him before he went far enough to involve himself seriously. Something led him to doubt the success of his project, and he came and consulted me on the subject. I satisfied him in ten minutes that it wouldn't do, and he at once abandoned it. Unfortunately, you arrived just at this time, and were made to bear the loss of his mistake."

"You are certainly not serious in what you say, Mr. Page!"

"I never was more serious in my life," returned the old gentleman.

"And you permitted me to be made the victim, upon your own acknowledgment, of a shameful swindle, and did not expend even a breath to save me!"

"I am not used to be spoken to in that way, young man," replied Mr. Page, coldly, and with a slightly offended air. "Nor am I in the habit of forcing my advice upon everybody."

"If you saw a man going blindfold towards the brink of a precipice, wouldn't you force your advice upon him?"

"Perhaps I might. But as you were not going blindfold over a precipice, I did not see that it was my business to interfere."

A cutting reply was on the lips of Jordan, but a thought of Edith cooled him off suddenly, and he in a milder and more respectful tone of voice, "I should be glad, Mr. Page, if you would demonstrate the error under which I have been labouring in regard to this business. If there is an error, I wish to see it; and can see it as quickly as any one, if it really exists, and the proper means of seeing it are furnished."

The change in the young man's manner softened Mr. Page, and he sat down, pencil in hand, and by the aid of the answers which the actual experience of Jordan enabled him to give, showed him, in ten minutes, that the more land he cleared and the more logs he sawed up, the poorer he would become.

"And you knew all this before?" said Jordan.

"Certainly I did. In fact, I built the saw-mill owned by Tompkins, and after sinking a couple of thousand dollars, was glad to get it off of my hands at any price. Tompkins makes a living with it, and nothing more. But then he is his own engineer, manager, clerk, and almost every thing else, and lives with the closest economy in his family—much closer than you or I would like to live."

"And you let me go on blindly and ruin myself, when a word from you might have saved me!"

There was something indignant in the young man's manner.

"You didn't consult me on the subject. It is not my place to look after everybody's business; I have enough to do to take care of my own concerns."

Both were getting excited. Jordan retorted still more severely, and then they parted in anger, each feeling that he had just cause to be offended.

On the next day, Jordan, who was too well satisfied that Mr. Page was right, stopped his mill, discharged his hands, and sold his oxen. On looking over his accounts, he found that he was over a thousand dollars in debt: In order to pay this, he sold the balance of his land, and then advertised his saw-mill for sale in all the county papers, and in the State Gazette.

Meantime, the suit which had been instituted on the note given to Barnaby came up for trial, and Jordan made an effort to defend it on the plea that value had not been received. His fifty acres of land were gone, and all that remained of his six thousand dollars, were a half-weatherboarded, frame building, called a saw-mill, in which were a secondhand steam-engine, some rough gearing, and a few saws. This stood in the centre of a small piece of ground—perhaps the fourth of an acre—upon which there was the moderate annual rent of one hundred dollars! More than the whole building, leaving out the engine, would sell for.

After waiting for two months, and not receiving an offer for the mill, he sold the engine for a hundred and fifty dollars, and abandoned the old frame building in which it had stood, to the owner of the land for rent, on condition of his cancelling the lease, that had still three years and a half to run.

His defence of the suit availed nothing. Judgment was obtained upon the note, an execution issued, and, as there was no longer any property in the young man's possession, his person was seized and thrown into the county prison.

From the time old Mr. Page considered himself insulted by Jordan, all intercourse between them had ceased. The latter had not considered himself free to visit any longer at his house, and therefore no meeting between him and Edith had taken place for three months.

The cause of so sudden a cessation of her lover's visits, all unknown to Edith, was a great affliction to the maiden. Her father noticed that her countenance wore a troubled aspect, and that she scarcely tasted food when at the table. This did not, in any way, lessen the number of his self-reproaches for having suffered a young man to ruin himself, when a word from him might have saved him.

Edith was paying a visit to a friend one day, the daughter of a lawyer. While conversing, the friend said—

"Poor Jordan? Have you heard of his misfortunes?"

"No! What are they?" And Edith turned pale. The friend was not aware of her interest in him.

"He was terribly cheated in some saw-mill property he bought," she made answer, "and has since lost every dollar he had. Yesterday he was sent to prison for debt which he is unable to pay."

Edith heard no more, but, starting up, rushed from the house, and flew, rather than walked, home. Her father was sitting in his private office when she entered with pale face and quivering lips. Uttering an exclamation of surprise and alarm, he rose to his feet. Edith fell against him, sobbing as she did so, while the tears found vent, and poured over her cheeks—

"Oh, father! He is in prison!"

"Who? Jordan?"

"Yes," was the maiden's lowly-murmured reply.

"Good heavens! Is it possible?"

With this exclamation, Mr. Page pushed his daughter from him, and leaving the house instantly, took his way to the office of the attorney who had conducted the suit in favour of Barnaby.

"I will go bail for this young man whom you have thrown into prison," said he as soon as he met the lawyer.

"Very well, Mr. Page. We will take you. But you will have to pay the amount—he has nothing."

"I said I would go his bail," returned the old man, impatiently.

In less than twenty minutes, Mr. Page entered the apartment where the young man was confined. Jordan looked at him angrily. He had just been thinking of the cruel neglect to warn him of his errors, of which Mr. Page had been guilty, and of the consequences, so disastrous and so humbling to himself.

"You are at liberty," said the old gentleman, as he approached him and held out his hand.

Jordan stood like one half-stupified, for some moments.

"I have gone your security, my young friend," Mr. Page added kindly. "You are at liberty."

"*You* my security!" returned Jordan, taking the offered hand, but not grasping it with a hearty pressure. He felt as if he couldn't do that. "I am sorry you have done so," said he, after a slight pause—"I am not worth a dollar, and you will have my debt to pay."

"It's no time to talk about that now, Mr. Jordan. I have gone your security, because I thought it right to do so. Come home with me, and we will soon arrange all the rest."

Jordan felt passive. A child could have led him anywhere. He did not refuse to go with Mr. Page.

Edith was sitting in the room where her father left her, when the opening of the door caused her to start. There was an exclamation of delight and surprise; a movement forward, and then deep blushes threw a crimson veil over the maiden's face, as she sank back in her chair and covered her face with her hands. But the tears could not be hidden; they came trickling through her fingers.

Enough, further to say, that within two months there was a wedding at the house of Mr. Page, and Edith was the bride.

It has been noticed since, that the old gentleman does not stand so much on his dignity when there is a chance of doing good by volunteering a word of advice in season. "Had I been consulted," is a form of speech which he is now rarely, if ever known to use.

THE MISTAKES OF A "RISING FAMILY."

MR. MINTURN was a rising man; that is, he was gaining money and reputation in his profession. That he felt himself rising, was clearly apparent to all who observed him attentively. His good lady, Mrs. Minturn, was also conscious of the upward movement, and experienced a consequent sense of elevation. From the height they had gained in a few years, it was but natural for them to cast their eyes below, and to note how far beneath them were certain individuals with whom they had once been on a level. The observation of this fact as naturally created an emotion of contempt for these individuals as inferiors.

Among those ranging below the Minturns,—in their estimation,—was a family named Allender. Mr. Allender was, or had been, a merchant, and was highly esteemed by all who knew him, as a gentleman and a man of fine intelligence. He and Minturn started together in life; the one as a lawyer, and the other as a merchant. Possessing some capital, Mr. Allender was able, in commencing business, to assume a comfortable style of living in his family, while Minturn, who had nothing but his profession to depend upon, and that at the time of his marriage a very small dependence, was compelled to adopt, in his domestic relations, a very humble scale.

Having been well acquainted, for some years, with Mr. Minturn, Mr. Allender, soon after the marriage of the former, called upon him with his wife. The visit was promptly returned, and from that time the two families kept up intimate relations. The Minturns lived in a small house, in a retired street, for which they paid the annual rent of one hundred and seventy-five dollars. Their house was furnished with exceeding plainness, and their only domestic was a stout girl of fourteen. The Allenders, on the other hand, lived in a fashionable neighbourhood, so called. For their house, which was handsomely furnished, they paid a rent of four hundred dollars; and lived in what the Minturns thought to be great elegance. And so it was, in contrast with their style of living. Mrs. Minturn felt quite proud of having such acquaintances, and of being able to visit familiarly in such good society as was to be found at the house of Mr. and Mrs. Allender. You could not be in her company for ten minutes, at any time, without hearing some allusion to the Allenders. What they said, was repeated as oracular; and to those who had never been in their house, Mrs. Minturn described the elegance of every thing pertaining thereto, in the most graphic manner.

Well, as time went on, Mr. Minturn, by strict devotion to business, gradually advanced himself in his profession. At the end of four or five years, he was able to move into a larger house and to get better furniture.

Still, every thing was yet on an inferior scale to that enjoyed by Mr. Allender, to whose family his own was indebted for an introduction into society, and for an acquaintance with many who were esteemed as valued friends.

Ten years elapsed, and the Minturns were on a level with the Allenders, as far as external things were concerned. The lawyer's business had steadily increased, but the merchant had not been very successful in trade, and was not esteemed, in the community, a rising man. No change in his style of living had taken place since he first became a housekeeper; and his furniture began, in consequence, to look a little dingy and old-fashioned. This was particularly observed by Mrs. Minturn, who had, at every upward movement,—and three of these movements had already taken place,—furnished her house from top to bottom.

Five years more reversed the relations between to families. The Minturns still went up, and the Allenders commenced going down. One day, about this time, Mr. Minturn came home from his office, and said to his wife:

"I've got bad news to tell you about our friends the Allenders."

"What is that?" inquired Mrs. Minturn, evincing a good deal of interest, though not exactly of the right kind.

"He's stopped payment."

"What?"

"He failed to meet his notes in bank yesterday, and to-day, I understand, he has called his creditors together."

"I'm sorry to hear that, really," said Mrs. Minturn. "What is the cause?"

"I believe his affairs have been getting involved for the last four or five years. He does not seem to possess much business energy."

"I never thought there was a great deal of life about him."

"He's rather a slow man. It requires more activity and energy of character than he possesses to do business in these times. Men are getting too wide awake. I'm sorry for Allender. He's a good-hearted man—too good-hearted, in fact, for his own interest. But, it's nothing more than I expected."

"And I am sorry for poor Mrs. Allender," said his wife. "What a change it will be for her! Ah, me! Will they lose every thing?"

"I have no means of knowing at present. But I hope not."

"Still, they will have to come down a great way."

"No doubt of it."

A week passed, after news of Mr. Allender's business disaster had reached the ears of Mrs. Minturn, and in that time she had not called to see her friend in distress. Each of these ladies had a daughter about the same age; and that age was fifteen.

"Where are you going, Emeline?" asked Mrs. Minturn of her daughter, who came down, with her bonnet on, one afternoon about this time.

"I'm going to run around and see Clara Allender," was replied.

"I'd rather you wouldn't go there, just now," said the mother.

"Why not?" asked Emeline.

"I have my reasons for it," returned Mrs. Minturn.

Emeline looked disappointed. She was much attached to Clara, who was a sweet-tempered girl, and felt a week's absence from her as a real privation. Observing the disappointment of Emeline, Mrs. Minturn said, a little impatiently:

"I think you might live without seeing Clara every day. For some time past, you have been little more than her shadow. I don't like these girlish intimacies; they never come to any good."

Tears were in Emeline's eyes as she turned from her mother and went back to her room.

Mr. Allender, at the age of forty, found himself unable, through the exhaustion of his means, to continue in business. He would have resigned every thing into the hands of his creditors before suffering a protest, had he not failed to receive an expected payment on the day of his forced suspension. When he did call together the men to whom he was indebted, he rendered them up all his effects, and in all possible ways aided in the settlement of every thing. The result was better than he had anticipated. No one lost a dollar; but he was left penniless. Just then, the president of one of the Marine Insurance Companies resigned his office, and Mr. Allender was unanimously chosen to fill his place. The salary was two thousand dollars. This was sufficient to meet the expense at which his family had been living. So there was no change in their domestic economy. This being the case, the Minturns had no good reason for cutting the acquaintance of their old friends, much as they now felt disposed to do so. The family visiting, however, was far from being as frequent and as familiar as in former times.

Still, on the part of the Minturns the movement was upward, while the Allender's retained their dead level. The lawyer, who was a man of talents and perseverance, and withal not over scrupulous on points of abstract morality, gained both money and reputation in his profession, and was at length known as one of the most acute and successful men at the bar. At last, he was brought forward by one of the political parties as a candidate for a seat in Congress, and elected.

If Mrs. Minturn's ideas of her own elevation and importance in the social world had been large, they were now increased threefold. A winter's residence at the seat of government,—during which time she mingled freely with the little great people who revolve around certain fixed stars that shine with varied light in the political metropolis,—raised still higher the standard of self-estimation. Her daughter Emeline, now a beautiful and accomplished young lady, accompanied her mother wherever she went, and attracted a large share of attention. Among those who seemed particularly pleased with Emeline was a young man, a member of Congress from New York, who belonged to a wealthy and distinguished family, and who was himself possessed of brilliant talent, that made him conspicuous on the floor of Congress, even among men of long-acknowledged abilities. His name was Erskine.

Soon after meeting with the Hon. Mr. Erskine, Mrs. Minturn felt a strong desire to bring him to the feet of her daughter. He presented just the kind of alliance she wished for Emeline. In imagination she soon began to picture to herself the elevated and brilliant position her child would occupy as the wife of Erskine, and she resolved to leave no means untried for the accomplishment of her wishes. Accordingly, she was particularly attentive to the young man whenever thrown into his company; and sought, by flattering his self-love, to make him feel in the best possible humour with himself while in her society. In this way she succeeded in drawing him frequently to her side, where Emeline was always to be found. A sprightly, well-educated, and finely accomplished girl, Emeline soon interested the young M. C.; and he showed her, as has been said, a good deal of attention during the winter, and Mrs. Minturn flattered herself that her daughter had made a conquest.

When the session of Congress closed, the Minturns returned home in the enjoyment of a much higher opinion of themselves than they had ever before entertained, and quite disposed to be rather more choice than before in regard to their visiting acquaintance. A few days after their reappearance in old circles, a card of invitation to meet some friends at the house of Mr. and Mrs. Allender was received. It extended to themselves and their eldest daughter, Emeline. Mrs. Minturn handed the card to her husband on his return from his office in the evening.

"What is this?" he asked, on taking it. "Ah, indeed!" he added, in rather an equivocal voice, on perceiving its tenor. "Are you going?"

"I rather think not."

"Just as you say about it," remarked the acquiescing husband.

"The truth is," said Mrs. Minturn, "a regard for our position makes it necessary for us to be more select in our acquaintances. I don't wish Emeline to be on terms of intimacy with Clara Allender any longer. There is too great a difference in their social relations. As people are judged by the company they keep, they should be a little choice in their selection. I like Mrs. Allender very well in her place. She is a good, plain, common-sense sort of a woman, but she occupies a grade below us; and we should remember and act upon this for the sake of our children, if for nothing else."

"No doubt you are right," replied Mr. Minturn. "Mr. Allender has neither energy of character nor enterprise; he, therefore, occupies a dead level in society. At that level he cannot expect every one else to remain."

"Not us, at least."

"No."

"Clara called to see Emeline yesterday. I saw her in the parlour, and asked her to excuse Emeline, as she was a little indisposed. It is true, I had to fib a little. But that was better than a renewal of an acquaintance that ought now to cease. She seemed a little hurt, but I can't help it."

"Of course not. I am sorry, for their sakes, that we must give up the acquaintance. No loss can come to us, as we have more friends, now, than are just convenient."

"It would help Clara a good deal," remarked Mrs. Minturn, "to mingle in our circle. Her mother feels this, and, therefore, does not wish to give us up. I've not the least doubt but this party is made on our account. It won't do, however; they will have to let us go."

"It will be sufficient to send our regrets," said Mr. Minturn.

"We'd better not even do that," replied his wife. "That will indicate a wish to retain the acquaintance, and we have no such desire. Better sever the relation at once and be done with the matter. It is unpleasant at least, and there is no use in prolonging disagreeable sensations."

"Be it so, then," remarked Mr. Minturn, rising; and so the thing was decided.

Mrs. Minturn had lapsed into a small mistake touching the reason that induced Mr. and Mrs. Allender to give an entertainment just at that time. It was not in honour of their return from Washington, and designed to unite the families in a firmer union; no, a thought like this had not entered the mind of the Allenders. The honour was designed for another—even for the Hon. Mr. Erskine, who was the son of one of Mr. Allender's oldest and most valued friends, whom he had not seen for many years, yet with whom he had enjoyed an uninterrupted correspondence. On his return home, Mr. Erskine remained a few days in the city, as much to see Mr. Allender as for any thing else, his father having particularly desired him to do so. He had never met Mr. Allender before, but was charmed with his gentlemanly character and fine intelligence at the first interview, and still more pleased with him at each subsequent meeting. With Mrs. Allender he was also pleased; but, most of all, with Clara. About the latter there was a charm that won his admiration. She was beautiful; but how different her beauty from that of the brilliant belles who had glittered in the gay circles of fashion he had just left! It was less the beauty of features than that which comes through them, as a transparent medium, from the pure and lovely spirit within. Erskine had been more than pleased with Miss Minturn; but he thought of her as one in a lower sphere while in the presence of Clara, who, like a half-hidden violet, seemed all unconscious of beauty or fragrance.

Yes, it was for Mr. Erskine that the party was given, and in order to introduce him to a highly refined and intellectual circle, of which Mr. Allender and his wife notwithstanding external reverses, were still the centre. Not from any particular pleasure that was expected to be derived from the company of the Minturns, were they invited; for, in going up, they had changed so for the worse, that their society had become irksome, if not offensive. But, for the sake of old friendship, they were included. But they did not come; and no one missed them.

On the next day, Mr. Erskine called upon Mrs. Minturn and her daughter, as he intended leaving the city in the afternoon.

"We looked for you all last evening," said Mrs. Minturn. "Why did you not call around?"

"I was at a select party last night," replied the young man.

"Were you, indeed?"

"Yes. At Mr. Allender's. Do you know the family?"

"At Allender's!" The tone of surprise, not altogether unmingled with contempt, with which this was uttered by Mrs. Minturn, put Erskine a little on his guard.

"Do you know them?" he asked, with some gravity of manner.

"Not very intimately. We had some acquaintance in former years, but we have broken it off. They sent us cards of invitation, but we did not notice them."

"What is their standing?"

"Not high. I believe none of our first people visit them."

"Ah!"

"Who was there?" asked Emeline.

The tone in which this was spoken caused Mr. Erskine to turn and look somewhat closely into the young lady's face, to mark its expression. She had never appeared less lovely in his eyes.

"Not a great many," he replied.

"I suppose not," said Mrs. Minturn.

"It was a select party," remarked the young man.

"And select enough, no doubt, you found it."

"You speak truly. I have never been in one more so," replied Erskine.

"You have not answered my question as to who were there," said Emeline.

"Young ladies, do you mean?"

"Yes, young ladies."

"Do you know Miss B——?"

"I have no particular acquaintance with her. But she was not there!"

"Oh, yes, she was. And so was her father, General B——."

"You astonish me!" said Mrs. Minturn. "Certainly you are in error."

"I believe not. I had a good deal of interesting conversation with General B——, who is well acquainted with my father."

"Who else was there?"

"Senator Y——, and his beautiful niece, who created such a sensation in Washington last winter. She and Miss Allender, who is, it strikes me, a charming girl, seemed delighted with each other, and were side by side most of the evening. They sang together many times with exquisite effect. Then there were Mr. and Mrs. T——, Mr. and Mrs. R——, Miss Julia S——, and Miss G——."

All these belonged to a circle yet above that in which the Minturns had moved.

"I am astonished," said Mrs. Minturn, but poorly concealing her mortification. "I had no idea that the Allenders kept such company. How did you happen to be invited?"

"Mr. Allender is one of my father's oldest and most valued friends. I called at his desire, and found both him and his family far above the 'common run' of people. I do not in the least wonder at the class of persons I met at their house. I am sorry that you have been led so far astray in your estimation of their characters. You never could have known them well."

"Perhaps not," said Mrs. Minturn, in a subdued voice. "Did you hear us asked for?" she ventured to add. "We were invited, as I mentioned, and would have gone, but didn't expect to find any there with whom it would be agreeable to associate."

This remark did not in the least improve the matter in the eyes of Mr. Erskine, who now understood the Minturns rather better than before. A feeling of repugnance took the place of his former friendly sentiments; and in a briefer time than he had intended, he brought his visit to a close, and bade them good morning.

What was now to be done? The Minturns had fallen into an error, which must, if possible, be repaired. The Allenders were of far more consequence than they had believed, and their estimation of them rose correspondingly. A note of regret at not being able to attend the party, in consequence of a previous engagement, was written, and this enclosed in another note, stating that in consequence of the neglect of a servant, it had not been delivered on the day before. Both were despatched within half an hour after Mr. Erskine left the house.

On the day after, Mrs. Minturn and her daughter called at Mrs. Allender's, and offered verbal regrets at not having been able to attend the party.

"We wanted to come very much, but both Emeline and I were so much indisposed, that the doctor said we mustn't think of going out,"—forgetting at the moment the tenor of the note she had written only the day before. But scarcely were the words out of her mouth, when a glance of uneasy surprise from Emeline brought a recollection of this fact, and caused the blood to mount to her face.

A sudden change in the manner of Mrs. Allender was conclusive evidence that she, too, was laying side by side the two conflicting statements.

"But even," added Mrs. Minturn, in a voice that betrayed some disturbance of mind, "if we had not been indisposed, a previously made engagement would have been in the way of a pleasure that we shall always regret having lost. You had a highly select party, I understood."

"Only a few old and much esteemed friends, that we invited to meet a gentleman who was passing through the city, whose father and Mr. Allender are old acquaintances."

"The Hon. Mr. Erskine, you mean," said Mrs. Minturn, whose vanity led her to betray herself still more.

"Yes. Have you met him?"

"Oh, yes," was replied with animation. "We were very intimate at Washington. He showed Emeline very particular attentions."

"Ah! I was not aware that you knew him."

"Intimately. He called to see us yesterday, on the eve of his departure for New York."

"Oh, mother!" exclaimed Emeline, as soon as they had stepped beyond the street-door, on leaving the house of Mrs. Allender, "why did you say any thing at all about Mr. Erskine, and especially after blundering so in the matter of apology? She'll see through it all, as clear as daylight. And won't we look beautiful in her eyes? I'm mortified to death!"

"I don't know what came over me," returned the mother, with evident chagrin. "To think that I should have been so beside myself!"

So much mortified were both the mother and daughter, on reflection, that they could not venture to call again upon Mrs. Allender and Clara, who did not return the last visit. And the intimacy from that time was broken off.

The next winter came round, and the Minturns repaired again to Washington. Emeline had hoped to receive a letter from Mr. Erskine, whom she half believed to be in love with her; but no such desired communication came. But she would meet him at the Capitol; and to that time of meeting she looked forward with feelings of the liveliest interest. On arriving in Washington, at the opening of the session, she repaired, on the first day, to the Capitol. But much to her disappointment, a certain member from New York was not in his place.

"Where is Mr. Erskine," she asked of his colleague, whom she met in the evening.

"Has not arrived yet," was replied. "Will probably be along to-morrow or next day. He stopped in your city as he came along; and I shrewdly suspect that he had in contemplation a very desperate act."

"Indeed! What was that?" returned Emeline, endeavouring to appear unconcerned.

"Taking to himself a wife."

"You surprise me," said the young lady. "Who is the bride?"

"I don't know. He said nothing to me on that subject. Others, who appear to be in the secret, aver that his detention is occasioned by the cause I have alleged."

It required a strong effort on the part of Miss Minturn to keep from betraying the painful shock her feelings had sustained. She changed the subject as quickly as possible.

On the next day, it was whispered about that Mr. Erskine had arrived in company with his newly-made bride.

"Who is she?" asked both Mrs. Minturn and her daughter; but no one to whom they applied happened to know. Those who had seen her pronounced her very beautiful. Two days passed, and then a bridal party was given, to which Mrs. Minturn and Emeline were invited. They had been sitting in the midst of a large company for about ten minutes, their hearts in a flutter of anticipation, when there was a slight movement at the door, and then Mr. Erskine entered with his bride upon his arm. One glance sufficed for Mrs. Minturn and her daughter—it was Clara! While others were pressing forward to greet the lovely bride, they, overcome with disappointment, and oppressed by mortification, retired from the room, and, ordering their carriage, left the house unobserved.

Up to this day, they have never sought to renew the acquaintance.

THE MEANS OF ENJOYMENT.

ONE of the most successful merchants of his day was Mr. Alexander. In trade he had amassed a large fortune, and now, in the sixtieth year of his age, he concluded that it was time to cease getting and begin the work of enjoying. Wealth had always been regarded by him as a means of happiness; but, so fully had his mind been occupied in business, that, until the present time, he had never felt himself at leisure to make a right use of the means in his hands.

So Mr. Alexander retired from business in favour of his son and son-in-law. And now was to come the reward of his long years of labour. Now were to come repose, enjoyment, and the calm delights of which he had so often dreamed. But, it so happened, that the current of thought and affection which had flowed on so long and steadily was little disposed to widen into a placid lake. The retired merchant must yet have some occupation. His had been a life of purposes, and plans for their accomplishment; and he could not change the nature of this life. His heart was still the seat of desire, and his thought obeyed, instinctively, the heart's affection.

So Mr. Alexander used a portion of his wealth in various ways, in order to satisfy the ever active desire of his heart for something beyond what was in actual possession. But, it so happened, that the moment an end was gained, the moment the bright ideal became a fixed and present fact, its power to delight the mind was gone.

Mr. Alexander had some taste for the arts. Many fine pictures already hung upon his walls. Knowing this, a certain picture-broker threw himself in his way, and, by adroit management and skilful flattery, succeeded in turning the pent-up and struggling current of the old gentleman's feelings and thoughts in this direction. The broker soon found that he had opened a new and profitable mine. Mr. Alexander had only to see a fine picture, to desire its possession; and to desire was to have. It was not long before his house was a gallery of pictures.

Was he any happier? Did these pictures afford him a pure and perennial source of enjoyment? No; for, in reality, Mr. Alexander's taste for the arts was not a passion of his mind. He did not love the beautiful in the abstract. The delight he experienced when he looked upon a fine painting, was mainly the desire of possession; and satiety soon followed possession.

One morning, Mr. Alexander repaired alone to his library, where, on the day before, had been placed a new painting, recently imported by his friend the picture-dealer. It was exquisite as a work of art, and the biddings for it had been high. But he succeeded in securing it for the sum of two thousand dollars. Before he was certain of getting this picture, Mr. Alexander would linger before it, and study out its beauties with a delighted appreciation. Nothing in his collection was deemed comparable therewith. Strangely enough, after it was hung upon the walls of his library, he did not stand before it for as long a space as five minutes; and then his thoughts were not upon its beauties. During the evening that followed, the mind of Mr. Alexander was less in repose than usual. After having completed his purchase of the picture, he had overheard two persons, who were considered autocrats in taste, speaking of its defects, which were minutely indicated. They likewise gave it as their opinion that the painting was not worth a thousand dollars. This was throwing cold water on his enthusiasm. It seemed as if a veil had suddenly been drawn from before his eyes. Now, with a clearer vision, he could see faults where, before, every defect was thrown into shadow by an all-obscuring beauty.

On the next morning, as we have said, Mr. Alexander entered his library, to take another look at his purchase. He did not feel very happy. Many thousands of dollars had he spent in order to secure the means of self-gratification; but the end was not yet gained.

A glance at the new picture sufficed, and then Mr. Alexander turned from it with an involuntary sigh. Was it to look at other pictures? No. He crossed his hands behind him, bent his eyes upon the floor, and for the period of half an hour, walked slowly backwards and forwards in his library. There was a pressure on his feelings, he knew not why; a sense of disappointment and dissatisfaction.

No purpose was in the mind of Mr. Alexander when he turned from his library, and, drawing on his overcoat, passed forth to the street. It was a bleak winter morning, and the muffled pedestrians hurried shivering on their way.

"Oh! I wish I had a dollar."

These words, in the voice of a child, and spoken with impressive earnestness, fell suddenly upon the ears of Mr. Alexander, as he moved along the pavement. Something in the tone reached the old man's feelings, and he partly turned himself to look at the speaker. She was a little girl, not over eleven years of age, and in company with a lad some year or two older. Both were coarsely clad.

"What would you do with a dollar, sis?" replied the boy.

"I'd buy brother William a pair of nice woollen gloves, and a comforter, and a pair of rubber shoes. That's what I'd do with it. He has to go away, so early, in the cold, every morning; and he's 'most perished, I know, sometimes. Last night his feet were soaking with wet. His shoes are not good; and mother says she hasn't money to buy him a new pair just now. Oh, I wish I had a dollar!"

Instinctively Mr. Alexander's hand was in his pocket, and, a moment after, a round, bright silver dollar glittered in that of the girl.

But little farther did Mr. Alexander extend his walk. As if by magic, the hue of his feelings had changed. The pressure on his heart was gone, and its fuller pulses sent the blood bounding and frolicking along every expanding artery. He thought not of pictures nor possessions. All else was obscured by the bright face of the child, as she lifted to his her innocent eyes, brimming with grateful tears.

One dollar spent unselfishly, brought more real pleasure than thousands parted with in the pursuit of merely selfish gratification. And the pleasure did not fade with the hour, nor the day. That one truly benevolent act, impulsive as it had been, touched a sealed spring of enjoyment, and the waters that gushed instantly forth continued to flow unceasingly.

Homeward the old man returned, and again he entered his library. Choice works of art were all around him, purchased as a means of enjoyment.

They had cost thousands,—yet did they not afford him a tithe of the pleasure he had secured by the expenditure of a single dollar. He could turn from them with a feeling of satiety; not so from the image of the happy child whose earnestly expressed wish he had gratified.

And not alone on the pleasure of the child did the thoughts of Mr. Alexander linger. There came before his imagination another picture. He saw a poorly furnished room, in which were a humble, toiling widow and her children. It is keen and frosty without; and her eldest boy has just come home from his work, shivering with cold. While he is warming himself by the fire, his little sister presents him with the comforter, the thick gloves, and the overshoes, which his benevolence has enabled her to buy. What surprise and pleasure beam in the lad's face! How happy looks the sister! How full of a subdued and thankful pleasure is the mother's countenance.

And for weeks and months, did Mr. Alexander gaze, at times, upon this picture, and always with a warmth and lightness of heart unfelt when other images arose in his mind and obscured it.

And for a single dollar was all this obtained, while thousands and thousands were spent in the fruitless effort to buy happiness.

Strange as it may seem, Mr. Alexander did not profit by this lesson—grew no wiser by this experience. The love of self was too strong for him to seek the good of others, to bless both himself and his fellows by a wise and generous use of the ample means which Providence had given into his hands. He still buys pictures and works of art, but the picture in his imagination, which cost but a single dollar, is gazed at with a far purer and higher pleasure than he receives from his entire gallery of paintings and statues.

If Mr. Alexander will not drink from the sweet spring of true delight that has gushed forth at his feet, and in whose clear waters the sun of heavenly love is mirrored, we hope that others, wiser than he, will bend to its overflowing brim, and take of its treasures freely.

THE END.

CPSIA information can be obtained
at www.ICGtesting.com
Printed in the USA
LVHW030141271222
735871LV00001B/231